Fern Coppedge Found At Hot Dog Stand

October
Fern Isabel
Coppedge

16″ x 16″
Oil On
Canvas

(Story in
Chapter 2)

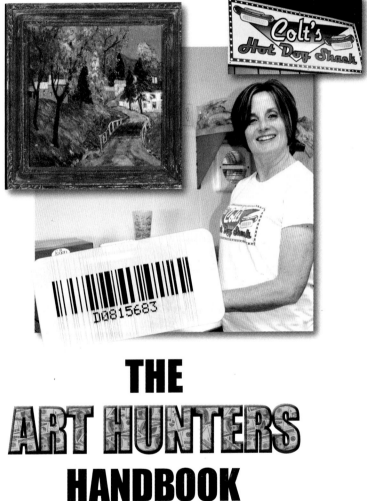

THE
ART HUNTERS
HANDBOOK

Les & Sue Fox

West Highland Fine Art & Publishing

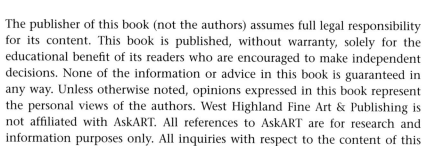

The publisher of this book (not the authors) assumes full legal responsibility for its content. This book is published, without warranty, solely for the educational benefit of its readers who are encouraged to make independent decisions. None of the information or advice in this book is guaranteed in any way. Unless otherwise noted, opinions expressed in this book represent the personal views of the authors. West Highland Fine Art & Publishing is not affiliated with AskART. All references to AskART are for research and information purposes only. All inquiries with respect to the content of this book should be directed only to the publisher.

Cover Photo: Joseph Decker *Ripening Pears*.
Gift of Ann and Mark Kington/The Kington Foundation and the Avalon Fund
Image courtesy National Gallery of Art, Washington.

Cover Photo / Frame: Krzysztof "Chris" Parypa Photography

Various photos in this book used with permission of the Artists Rights Society (ARS) New York: Josef Albers, Milton Avery, Willem DeKooning, Andre Derain, Lyonel Feininger, Lucio Fontana, Jacob Lawrence, Reginald Marsh, Pablo Picasso, Jackson Pollock and Kurt Schwitters.

Various photos in this book used with permission of VAGA (New York): Thomas Hart Benton, Will Barnet, Allan D'Arcangelo, Stuart Davis, Robert Motherwell, Kenneth Noland, Leon Polk Smith, Wayne Thiebaud and Tom Wesselmann.

Works by Norman Rockwell
Printed by permission of the Norman Rockwell Family Agency
Book Rights Copyright 2012 The Norman Rockwell Family Entities

Nighthawks by Edward Hopper
Collection of the Art Institute of Chicago
Photo Licensed By Corbis Images
© Francis G. Mayer/CORBIS

Book Design by James J. Ticchio / Direct Media Advertising

WEST HIGHLAND FINE ART & PUBLISHING, LLC

P.O. Box 36 • Midland Park, New Jersey 07432
© Copyright 2012 West Highland / Les and Sue Fox

MANUFACTURED IN THE UNITED STATES OF AMERICA

May, 2012 Edition - 10 9 8 7 6 5 4 3 2 1

ISBN #0615593906

Table of Contents

**Think Of The Art Hunters Handbook As A Lottery Ticket.
With Better Odds.**

THE ART HUNTERS HANDBOOK
Introduction: Luck vs. Skill

Turn this page and you will read the amazing story of someone who actually bought a $1,000,000 painting for $5! Realistically, this was an exceptionally lucky day. However, millions of people buy lottery tickets with 100-million-to-1 odds of winning the big prize. Maybe they will only win $1,000 to $10,000. The same thing is true with art. The odds of finding a $5,000 painting at a garage sale or flea market are pretty good. How do we know? Because *every month* dozens of people contact us with fresh finds. In 2011, a woman who owns a hot dog stand in North Carolina came across a painting by Fern Coppedge. We bought the painting with her, as partners, and sold it at auction for $30,000. (See Chapter 2.)

You can't change the odds of winning the lottery. Either you pick the right numbers or you don't. The good news is, you *can* change the odds of finding a valuable oil painting. You can read this book. You can look over our 120 *Artist Profiles*, whose paintings are often worth far more than you might guess. You can develop an eye for good art. If you make a serious effort to find auction quality art, at least you will *recognize* a valuable painting! This book will teach you a lot. It was written for people with the treasure hunting spirit: *Art Hunters!*

It is our objective to help you find valuable art. What's wrong with finding a $25,000 painting? Or a $3,000 painting? From our personal experience, and the true stories revealed in *The Art Hunters Handbook*, such discoveries happen all the time. It can happen to you. It will take education and dedication. But remember: Unlike winning the lottery, the odds of finding a million-dollar painting are based on both luck *and* skill.

Of the 240,000 artists on AskART.com, only 120 are showcased in this book. You've probably never heard of most of them, and you may be shocked by some of the "crazy" high prices people have paid at auction. We believe there are still millions of great paintings "hiding" in garages, attics and thrift shops all over America. Study the artists in this book. Armed with knowledge and information, your story could be in our next edition. Go for it!

Les and Sue Fox

CHAPTER 1

Ripening Pears:
From Garage Sale To Art Museum

JOSEPH DECKER

When Roger Leiter (not his real name) visited a Los Angeles garage sale in 2001, little did he know what he would discover. The amateur art collector, an unidentified movie and TV actor, found a painting wrapped in a blanket on a shelf. It was a beautiful oil on canvas of a leafy tree branch brimming with dozens of ripening yellow, green and red pears. Leiter was delighted. He was quoted a price of $5, paid in cash, and claimed his prize. The painting hung in his kitchen for three years. When he decided to re-frame it, he investigated the value before spending any more money. He Googled "J. Decker Artist." What popped up was Sotheby's, Christie's and a number of prestigious art galleries, including the Richard York Gallery in New York City. All were interested in acquiring original works by Decker.

Ripening Pears.

Leiter decided to keep his name confidential when he sold his Decker ("Ripening Pears") to the National Gallery Of Art in 2004 for more than $1,000,000 through the York Gallery. Meredith Ward, a successful art dealer, was working for York when she offered the painting to the museum. Unfortunately, both Ward and Milton Esterow of ARTNews, who broke the story to the media, couldn't give us the real name of the actor who bought *Ripening Pears*. In the hope of interviewing Mr. Leiter, we also contacted the National Gallery

Squirrel With Nuts. $165,000 (Sotheby's 1987)

of Art, and William H. Gerdts, an art expert and author of a 63-page essay titled "Joseph Decker - New Revelations" published in 1988. No luck in finding Leiter.

Ripening Pears is now in the National Gallery of Art in Washington, D.C., the best of three Deckers in their permanent collection. It is believed to have been exhibited at the National Academy of Design in 1884, the year it was painted, originally titled *A Good Season.* Because no photograph was published at the time, the beautiful 12" x 24" oil painting was re-titled *Ripening Pears.* The woman who sold it in 2001 claimed it was in her garage for 60 years. But where was the mysterious Decker from 1884 to 1941? We know that Joseph Decker died in obscurity in 1924. Therefore, if he still owned the painting in 1924, it resided "somewhere else" for the next 17 years until it arrived in the California garage as World War II began. Did a soldier wrap it in a blanket before leaving for War? On the discussion board of AskART.com, the great grand-daughter of Joseph Decker, Susan Lebell-Phillips, recalled paintings by the artist on her grandmother's wall, but has no idea what happened to them, or whether one might have been *Ripening Pears.*

What makes this painting by Joseph Decker so valuable? And why would someone sell a "masterpiece" for only $5? (Answer: Because it didn't look like a masterpiece.) We researched the value of paintings by Joseph Decker, now considered to be one of America's finest still life artists, through public auction records on AskART. An 8" x 14" oil painting titled *The Red Admiral* was sold at Sotheby's in 1989

The Red Admiral. $759,000 (Sotheby's 1989)

for $759,000. This remains the highest auction price ever paid for a Decker painting. *The Red Admiral* is actually a butterfly perched among a dozen yellow apples crowded on a tree branch, much like

Still Life With Sour Cherries. $203,750.
(Sotheby's 2001)

the famous pear painting.

In 1987, Sotheby's sold *Squirrel With Nuts* for $165,000. In 1990, they sold a 10" x 20" oil titled *Bough Of Pears* (vastly inferior to *Ripening Pears*), also for $165,000. In 2001, *Still Life With Sour Cherries* fetched $203,750, again at Sotheby's. In 2004, the same year the National Gallery bought *Ripening Pears*, Sotheby's put up another squirrel painting by Decker titled *A Great Feast* with an estimate of $500,000 to $700,000. It did not meet the minimum bid requirement and failed to sell. In 1999, Christie's was unable to sell a squirrel painting titled *Bonnie* (Decker's pet squirrel) for $250,000 to $350,000. Since 2006, when Eldred's Auctions sold *Still Life With Peaches* for $148,000, no other Decker has sold at auction for more than that, suggesting that Leiter got a good price for *Ripening Pears*. On the other hand, no one knows how much it might have brought at auction in 2004.

ABOUT THE ARTIST

Born in Germany in 1853, young Joseph Decker arrived in New York in 1867. He studied at the National Academy of Design in 1875, and at the Royal Academy in Munich in 1879. The 1880's were the artist's most successful decade. His work was exhibited and admired in Brooklyn and New York. It was collected by Thomas B. Clarke, the foremost collector of American art at the time. However, an influential art critic named Clarence Cook constantly made unfavorable comments about Decker, claiming his still lifes were inferior to acclaimed contemporary artists William Harnett and John F. Peto. This greatly depressed Joseph Decker, whose exhibitions faded in the 1890's. He virtually disappeared from the

Still Life With Peaches.
$148,000 (Eldreds 2006)

art scene in the early 20th century until his death in 1924.

The artist is now recognized for his brilliant and original "hard" still lifes (a photo-realist style), created earlier in his career, and his "soft" still lifes (a muted, atmospheric style) which were influenced by Impressionism in his later years. Decker had an affinity for fruit, and was able to capture strawberries, plums, grapes, apples, pears and cherries in a way that imbued them with personality. Joseph Decker married Amelia Wolf in the 1870's. She died in 1910. They had five children, two sons and three daughters.

Hard Candy. $116,000. (Christie's 2000)

One more curious note to this story. According to ARTNews, when asked if he still went to garage sales, Roger Leiter replied: "No, but I should go to more." Leiter claimed he bought a second painting at the same sale, also for $5. Could it be another Decker? Hmmm.

Cover Photo: Joseph Decker *Ripening Pears.*
Gift of Ann and Mark Kington/The Kington Foundation and the Avalon Fund
Image courtesy National Gallery of Art, Washington.

Art Just Around The Corner

As our version of Edward Hopper's iconic painting Nighthawks suggests, it's possible that you are "just around the corner" from a valuable painting without knowing it. Granted, you probably won't discover anything like Van Gogh's priceless "Starry Night" in your neighborhood. But you never know what you might find unless you hunt for it!

Introduction

If you flip back one page, you'll see we've made a small addition to Edward Hopper's 1942 painting: *Nighthawks.* The people in the diner are unaware of the masterpiece in the store window just around the corner. The point is: You, and millions of other art hunters, may not realize that there are valuable paintings in your own neighborhood. At flea markets, garage sales, estate sales, auctions and antique shops. Maybe on the wall of your grandmother's house. The amazing stories in this chapter are real. Thousands of people have discovered valuable art in unexpected places like Goodwill, the trash, schools, churches, attics and basements. Often, these paintings were in plain sight for decades (like *Ripening Pears*) but people mistakenly assumed they were copies or simply nothing special.

According to our research, there are an estimated 50 million undiscovered paintings in America worth hundreds to millions of dollars! Which someone, sooner or later, will cash in on. You may be asking yourself how there possibly could be *50 million* valuable paintings to search for? The answer is, most of the 240,000 artists listed on AskART created at least 1,000 paintings. That adds up to 240,000,000 (240 million) paintings! Only a fraction of these have been sold at auction. Many are in museums and private collections. But if just 20% are still "whereabouts unknown", that's 50 million paintings!

According to AskART CEO George Collins and his research team, there are 27,000 artists whose paintings have sold at auction for over $10,000, 16,000 artists whose paintings have sold for over $25,000, and 6,000 artists whose paintings have sold for over $100,000 apiece! Since 1992, more than 340,000 paintings have been auctioned for over $10,000, more than 194,000 paintings for over $25,000, and more than 67,000 paintings for over $100,000.

Isn't that more than enough paintings for you to find just one? Or maybe 5? Or how about 50 over the next ten years? We think that's possible, even *likely*. Remember, the title of this book is *The Art Hunters Handbook*. So it's our job to arm you with the knowledge to hunt down and capture these paintings. Hey, they're not going to knock on your door! And valuable paintings don't always "look valuable." The first step is to identify the artist and research his or her auction prices. Most artists were kind enough to sign their names for you, so it's easy to look them up.

"Goodwill (Store) Hunting"

Edouard Cortes

With many stores receiving 2,500 donations a day, Goodwill Industries continues to be a prime source of valuable art. The following story appeared in the Baltimore Sun on June 28, 2008: *"Had it not been for the discerning eyes of Goodwill store employees, the research skills of the store manager (Terri Tonelli in Easton, Maryland) and the help of a few art historians, the Parisian street scene painted by Impressionist Edouard-Leon Cortes might well be hanging today in a college dorm room."* "March aux Fleurs" *(The Flower Market)*, an early 20th century 9" x 13" oil painting by Cortes, might easily have passed for a souvenir shop repro. Instead, it wound up selling at Sotheby's on June 6, 2008 for $40,630.

Cortes' *Flower Market* is far from the only valuable painting discovered at Goodwill. A pair of 1895 Venetian canal oil paintings by Federico del Campo, a Peruvian-Italian artist, were

Federico del Campo Oils

Frank Benson Watercolor

Arthur Shilling Portrait
Photo courtesy of the Midland/
Penetanguishene Mirror.

Ellsworth Woodward

donated to a Goodwill in Toronto, Canada in 2009 and later sold at auction at Waddington's for $143,860. When a watercolor by Frank Benson, a famous American Impressionist, surfaced at a Goodwill in Oregon in 2006, it was auctioned on the Goodwill website with a starting bid of just $10. After bidders realized it was genuine the price rose (slightly) to $165,000. In January, 2009 a watercolor by Ellsworth Woodward, co-founder of Newcomb Pottery, brought $8,000 in a Goodwill auction in Nashville,Tennessee. And at a

Salvation Army thrift shop auction in Ontario, Canada, manager Lori Contois rescued a tiny portrait by Arthur Shilling. She was thrilled to raise $3,500 when research revealed that the artist was a highly collectible portrait painter. When was the last time you checked out your local Goodwill or Salvation Army shop? And don't forget to leave your name and number with the manager. If you're lucky enough to find a valuable painting at Goodwill, as many people have, feel free to share the windfall with the needy...after you sell. Just don't let someone else find it first!

Who Was Martin J. Heade?

Martin J. Heade

A surprising number of paintings by the American Hudson River School painter Martin Johnson Heade (1819-1904) have been discovered over the years. For many years, Heade's work, featuring hummingbirds, marshes and still lifes, was purchased mainly for decoration. In 2006, an 1880's painting of St. Augustine, Florida found in a Massachusetts attic was authenticated by Dr. Theodore Stebbins, Jr., an expert on Martin Heade. It was sold at a local auction in Fall River for $198,000. In 2004, another St. Augustine landscape, owned by a widow, sold for $218,500. The 6" x 12" painting had been purchased for several dollars in the 1970's by her late husband.

An un-named Heade salt marsh landscape titled *River Scene* was found in Boston in 2003. It was auctioned for $1,006,250 and is now on view at the Fogg Museum in Cambridge, Massachusetts. *Magnolias On A Gold Velvet Cloth,* bought for $30 with some used furniture, was used to cover a hole in the wall of an Indiana home for years. After recognizing the artist's style on the card of a board game called "Masterpiece", the owner contacted Kennedy Galleries in New York for an appraisal. The Museum of Fine Arts in Houston purchased the painting in 1999 for $1,250,000. *Two Magnolias On Blue Plush* was priced at $29 at a rummage sale in Wisconsin in 1989. It sold at Christie's in 1999 for $882,500 and is now in the collection of James W.

Heade: Hummingbird and Orchids

McGlothin of Bristol, Virginia. *Magnolia Blossoms on Blue Velvet* and *Cherokee Roses* were bought at an estate sale in Arizona for $60 in 1996. They were sold at Christie's later that year for $937,500 and

Heade: Marsh Landscape

$134,500 respectively. And finally, *Thunderstorm On Naragansett Bay* in the Amon Carter Museum in Fort Worth, Texas, was discovered in an antiques store in New York in 1943.

If you think these are the last Heades that will ever be found for

Heade: Magnolias On A Gold Velvet Cloth

a fraction of their value, think again. Heade created thousands of oil paintings! Only 200 have been sold at auction in the past 25 years. Hundreds more are in museums. Where are the rest? One might be in an attic in

Florida or Fall River, Massachusetts. Or at a garage sale just around the corner from you. Or sitting in a local consignment shop with a $100 price tag, or hanging on a family room wall, or in the back of a minivan on its way to a flea market. Theodore Stebbins, Jr., curator of art at Harvard University, suggests that this artist's work may continue to turn up in unlikely places. So keep your eyes open! If you find a Heade, and you need help with authentication or selling it at auction, please contact the authors of this book.

Thomas Gainsborough

Gainsborough Does eBay... And A $300 Raphael Sells For $37 Million!

A British dealer in Old Masters paintings, Philip Mould (co-host of the British TV show, *Fake or Fortune*) scours auctions hoping to identify an overlooked masterpiece. He once found a valuable 18th-century Thomas Gainsborough painting for under $200 on eBay. Possible value: $2 million.

This is quite unusual. But with patience and due diligence a knowledgeable art hunter can probably make a living buying paintings on eBay to sell in higher profile auctions. You can get a good idea of who's offering "tricky stuff" on eBay by reviewing the seller's current and recent auctions. Emailing questions about provenance and authenticity isn't foolproof, but it can't hurt. If you think you've found a good one, your best bet is to consult an expert.

Raphael's Lorenzo de'Medici

Even an old painting discovered in an attic may or may not be genuine. The same advice applies to Craigslist.

Sold At Christie's For $37.3 Million

Ira Spanierman owns New York's prestigious Spanierman Galleries. According to Bloomberg News, while poking around a New York City auction preview in 1968, Spanierman spied a painting of a bearded man in an ornate gold-and-raspberry vestment ascribed to an unknown artist of the Italian school. The young dealer, who had just founded the Spanierman Gallery, bid $325 for the canvas - and won it. In 1971, he succeeded in getting the 1518 painting authenticated by Raphael experts, who researched a label on the back of the painting saying that it had once been exhibited as a Raphael. International auction bidders at Christie's took the price of the painting to an astonishing $37.3 million on July 5, 2007. Asked why he waited 40 years to sell the painting, Spanierman commented: "I decided it was time to enjoy the money." Bravo!

Ira Spanierman

A Lost Michelangelo...Maybe?

Retired U.S. Air Force Lt. Colonel Martin Kober of Buffalo, New York may own a genuine 16th century painting of Jesus and Mary by Michelangelo. Yes, *the* Michelangelo! The artwork has been in his family since 1883, having passed through two Catholic Cardinals and ending up in the hands of a German Baroness named Villani. "The Mike" came to the Kober family after Villani willed it to her

lady-in-waiting Gertrude Young. Young was the sister-in-law of Kober's great-great-grandfather. She shipped the work to America in 1883. The painting was tucked behind Kober's parents' sofa for 27 years. When the Colonel retired in 2002, his father suggested checking out the tempera-on-wood masterpiece. If it was done by one of his students, it's still worth a million

dollars. But an original Michelangelo could be worth $300 million! This painting is the focus of a recent book titled "The Lost Michelangelos" by Antonio Forcellino, an art restorer and historian. The book claims that a May, 1545 letter unearthed in a Vatican library proves that Cardinal Reginald Pole, Henry VIII's cousin who served later as Archbishop of Canterbury, offered the *Pieta* to Italian Cardinal Ercole Gonzaga enroute to the Kober family centuries later. Infra-red and x-ray examination have revealed sketches and alterations attributed to Michalengelo. But the jury is still out. In October, 2011, Kober's painting was displayed at the Rome Foundation in Italy, alongside genuine Michelangelos and Raphaels. Stay tuned.

"The Kiss" Of Good Fortune

©Estate of Roy Lichtenstein

In March, 1965 a typist at Harry N. Abrams Publishing was invited to attend a "happening" sponsored by the Artists' Key Club, a group of pop artists. Participants met at the Hotel Chelsea in New York and invested $10 each in a lottery to win a key to a locker at Penn Station. Inside the lockers were 15 *original* works of art, including a Roy Lichtenstein and an Andy Warhol. The woman who won a 6"x6" crayon drawing by

Lichtenstein kept it for 45 years before discovering that she owned the *original drawing* for Roy's 1964 masterpiece *Kiss V*, now in the collection of former Microsoft executive Charles Simonyi. At the time, the drawing was worth $50. On May 11, 2011, Christie's sold *Drawing for Kiss V* for $2.1 million. Maybe there are still some unopened lockers in town!

Rec Room Treasures: A Pair Of Cropseys Sells For $840,000

Two 15" x 24" oil paintings hung for 80 years in the basement rec room of a man's childhood home in West Hartford, Connecticut over the ping-pong table alongside a paint-by-numbers picture by his older sister. After turning down an offer of $125 from a trash remover, the owner decided to get a free appraisal of what he thought  were cheap reproductions acquired by his Swedish grandmother, a seamstress for wealthy families on Fifth Avenue. Shocked to discover that the pair of landscapes were apparently done in the 1860's by Jasper Cropsey, a leading American Hudson River School painter, he had them authenticated by the Newington-Cropsey Foundation in Hastings-on-Hudson, N.Y. During his lifetime, Cropsey painted some 2,500 works of art. The ones found in the Connecticut basement, *Prospect Point, Niagara Falls In Winter* and *Autumn In America, Mt. Washington, New Hampshire* were offered

Autumn In America

Niagara Falls

for sale by the Clarke Auction Gallery of Larchmont, New York with an estimate of $40-$60,000 apiece on May 11, 2011. When the smoke cleared the winter scene had sold for $552,000, the autumn landscape for $288,000. "Thank God we didn't use them as a dart board," commented the owner.

Van Gogh Visits Wisconsin

A previously unknown 13" x 16" oil painting by Vincent Van Gogh was discovered in 1991 by an art hunter for Leslie Hindman, former host of HGTV's "At The Auction" and owner of Leslie Hindman Auctioneers in Chicago. According to the Chicago Tribune,

Still Life With Flowers was first identified as a Van Gogh by John Kuhn, a part-time dealer who spotted the painting on the wall of a suburban Milwaukee home while examining antique furniture. A middle-class couple had inherited it in the 1950's from Gebhard Adolf Guyer, a family relative and Swiss banker who collected art from 1910 to 1930. It isn't easy to authenticate an uncatalogued Van Gogh signed only with a "V" in the lower left corner. After obtaining permission from the owners, Hindman consulted the National Gallery of Art, who urged her to contact Han van Crimpen, senior research curator at the prestigious Rijksmuseum in Amsterdam. Without a doubt, said the Van Gogh authority, the work of art had been painted by Vincent in 1886. In March, 1991, Leslie Hindman auctioned the newly discovered Van Gogh for $1.43 million.

"Derby Day" Found In Beach House Breaks Auction Record

An anonymous resident of New England recently discovered a Victorian oil painting that had been hanging in his family's *unlocked* beach house for half a century. "The Derby Day" by William Powell Frith (English, 1819-1909) was sold at auction by Christie's London

for $818,350 on December 15, 2011, breaking the artist's previous auction record of $313,000. The 15x35 inch painting is actually a "sketch" for a larger masterpiece in the Tate Britain gallery in London. The painting was bought for a modest price by the seller's parents in the 1930's, a time when Victorian pictures were out of style. The controversial subject matter of "Derby Day" is a mixed crowd of the wealthy, gamblers, con men, acrobats and prostitutes, all attending the annual 1850's horse race at Epsom Downs.

From Trash To Cash: A Rufino Tamayo Mystery

In 2003, New Yorker Elizabeth Gibson was on her way to buy coffee on Manhattan's Upper West Side when she passed a large (38" x 51") *modern* oil painting sitting at the curb. Twenty minutes after she carried the piece back to her apartment, a garbage truck picked up the rest of the trash. "The painting had a strange power," said Gibson, who is not normally attracted to this type of art. *Tres Personajes* (1970) by the celebrated 20th century Mexican abstract artist Rufino Tamayo (see *Artist Profile* pages) was identified as a stolen work. The

painting had been purchased at Sotheby's in 1977 for $55,000 by a Houston businessman as a birthday present for his wife. It disappeared in 1987. Thanks to Elizabeth Gibson, it was returned to the owner, who re-sold it at Sotheby's in 2007 for $1,049,000. Gibson received a $15,000 reward from the owner and a finder's fee from Sotheby's. The FBI is still trying to find the art thief.

"Maybe You Should Go To Church More Often"

In 2002, a painting by the Irish artist Aloysius O'Kelly (1853-1936) was noticed on the rectory wall of St. Patrick's Church in Edinburgh. *Mass In A Connemara Church* is now considered to be of great religious significance, depicting the relationship

between a gifted priest and his followers. Appraised for over $1,000,000, it is currently on loan to the National Gallery Of Ireland. Another inspirational church story is the case of Christ Congregational Church in Silver Spring, Maryland. For decades, the church was short on money to fix up the old brick farmhouse used for retreats and summer camps. On September 15, 2007, that dream became a reality when they sold an 1870 landscape of *Mount Katahdin, Maine* by Virgil Macey Williams at Weschler's Auctions for $90,000. The dusty 26"x40" painting had been discovered in the farmhouse in 1973. Not looking very valuable, a church member took it home and slid it under a couch until she found the time to have it examined by a Smithsonian expert.

Art Discoveries On The Antiques Roadshow

Since it began broadcasting on PBS in 1997, The Antiques Roadshow has entertained millions with its expert appraisals of art and collectibles. Many people have been surprised, even flabberghasted, to discover how much some "stuff" is really worth. For example, a 1937 painting of the *Grand Coule Dam* by Clyfford Still (right), received as a housewarming gift in 1941, turned out to be worth $500,000. (Note: In 2011, one of Still's abstract expressionist paintings sold for $61 million!) Other paintings seen on the popular TV show include a James Beard worth $300,000-

$500,000, a Chuck Close worth $100,000-$150,000, a Jasper Cropsey worth $300,000, and a Norman Rockwell magazine cover illustration worth $500,000. Caution: Watching The Antiques Roadshow, which we love to do, is inspirational to the serious Art Hunter. In combination with this book, it could possibly make you run right out the door and start looking for a garage sale!

The Great Birger Sandzen Rescue

One of the most bizarre art auction tales of the 21st Century involves a pair of 48" x 60" Grand Canyon and Colorado landscapes by American Impressionist Birger Sandzen that were "rescued" twice. First, from the furnace room of a school, and second, from the auction block of Shannons, an auctioneer in Connecticut. In 2004, *A Mountain Symphony* and *Wild Horse Creek* were salvaged from the basement of Washington High School in Milwaukee, Wisconsin. Discovered during a tour

of the school, appraiser Peter Bentz valued the masterpieces at $500,000. With permission from the Washington High School council, principal Nancy Conner shipped the paintings to Gene Shannon, expecting the proceeds to help the struggling high school. But a complication arose. The Milwaukee School Board decided that Connor did not have the authority to sell the paintings. The board voted to rescind the auction contract.

A Mountain Symphony, 1927

Shannon demanded a cancellation fee of $105,000. The Milwaukee School Board sued Shannon. Shannon counter-sued. In the end, the Milwaukee School Board agreed to pay Shannons $29,500, and the paintings were returned to Wisconsin. The two huge oils had been sold directly by Sandzen to the Washington High graduating class of

Wild Horse Creek

1927 to encourage art appreciation. Susan Saller, an administrator with the Milwaukee school system, recently told us that the district currently has no plans to sell the paintings, which are now in storage. We offered to arrange for their public display in a museum. Ms. Saller thinks there could be many other Sandzen paintings waiting to be "re-discovered."

Time Stands Still: A Lost Portrait Of Marthe de Florian

In June, 2010, auctioneer Olivier Choppin-Janvry walked into a cobweb and dust-covered Paris apartment to take inventory of the deceased owner's possessions. Imagine his surprise when Janvry saw a previously unknown painting by Giovanni Boldini worth millions. *The year was 1940. Germany is marching through the French countryside, and French leaders sign their surrender.*

Pictures are taken of Adolf Hitler posing with the Eiffel Tower. Before all these events can transpire, the granddaughter of actress Marthe de Florian locks her furnished Parisian flat and flees the city for the South of France. Seventy years later, the woman passes away without ever having returned to her home. The rent has been paid, the contents untouched for seven decades. Marthe de Florian, lover of Italian portrait painter Giovanni Boldini (as well as the Prime Minister of France) lived there when the portrait was painted. Racy love letters tucked away in the drawers led to the discovery of a book by Boldini's widow which mentioned the portrait, painted in 1898 when de Florian was 24. Mystery solved. In September, 2010, the portrait of Marthe deFlorian enshrouded in a pale pink mousseline evening dress, was sold at a feverish auction at Drouot Saleshouse in Paris for $2.9 million.

"The Afghan-Attleboro Connection"

Afghans, a 7 by 10 foot masterpiece by the Russian Neo-Classical artist Alexandre Iacovleff, is another controversial painting which resided in a school for many years before its value was realized. In 2007, the committee of the Community School in North Attleboro, Massachusetts attempted to auction *Afghans* through Sotheby's, who recently sold an Iacovleff for $3.6 million. The painting, which depicts Afghan tribesmen, could fetch $2 million. But not so fast, folks. In 1951, William Charles Thompson, nephew of Robert Vose of the Vose Gallery in Boston, generously hung the painting in the school's auditorium. However, there is no paperwork

as to whether *Afghans* was an "outright gift" or a "public charitable trust." School Committee member Anthony Caicia has suggested that the painting should be returned to the grandson of the donor, Gregory Smith, who says his grandfather wanted the painting to be hung permanently in the school. While all of this is sorted out, possibly in court, Sothebys has had custody of it for 5 years.

Couch Potato Finds Lost Masterpiece

A Berlin student who bought a beat-up second-hand sofa bed at a flea market found out she'd been sleeping on a valuable baroque painting hidden inside. Michaela Derra, a spokeswoman for the

auction house Ketterer Kunst in Hamburg revealed the story when the painting was sold for $27,500 in October, 2007. Experts believe the 10"x15" oil on slate titled *Preparations For The Flight To Egypt* was painted between 1605 and 1610 by an unknown artist with ties to the Venetian painter Carlo Saraceni.

Interior Designer Gets A Bargain For 50 Cents

When Louise Camellerie stopped to browse boxes of "stuff " at a yard sale in Huntington Station, New York, she wasn't planning to find anything exciting. *Country Road,* a 10x12 oil on board by American Impressionist Antonio Cirino, had a 1920's Salmagundi Club label on the back with the original price tag of $25. But the seller gladly sold it to Louise for half a dollar because it didn't look like much. Maybe not, but even small paintings by this Rhode Island artist sell for $1,000. The new owner has no interest in selling her beautiful little gem.

Author Les Fox with Cirino owner

Fern Coppedge Turns Up At Hot Dog Stand

Alison Bledsoe

Alison Bledsoe was putting mustard on one of her signature "Southern Dogs" when a man walked up with a 16"x16" oil painting titled *October* by Fern Isabel Coppedge, the famous New Hope, PA Impressionist. "I think this is a good one," he said, referring to the dirty but colorful landscape. Alison bought the painting, contacted Les and Sue Fox, and made an "Art Auction Partnership" deal to sell it with

Authors Les and Sue Fox (with Bruno) consign Fern Coppedge to auction with Alasdair Nichol at Freeman's Auctioneers

Winter, Point Pleasant was discovered in an attic in Florida. *From the Authors collection.*

Freeman's in Philadelphia (America's oldest auction house). The pre-sale estimate was $12,000 to $18,000. On December 4, 2011, the professionally cleaned *October* was sold for $29,800. It may be a while until Alison interrupts her booming hot dog business in North Carolina to scoop up another fabulous work of art. Yet each year we are offered 10 to 20 original paintings by the prolific and talented Fern Coppedge.

Frieseke's "Olive Trees" Bought For $100, Goes To Auction (Twice)

Purchased for peanuts at a yard sale, *Olive Trees, Cagnes* was painted in France circa 1920 by American Impressionist Frederick Frieseke. Considering that the artist's work has sold for as much as $2.5 million, and paintings similar to *Olive Trees* for $100,000, why did it fail to sell in a Skinner's auction in Boston in early 2011 for

Olive Trees by Frieseke

Olive Trees by Van Gogh

$50,000? The painting was authenticated by Frieseke expert Nicholas Kilmer. It has an exciting story, and it sort of looks like a Van Gogh. The 25"x30" two-sided painting was first estimated to bring $50-$70,000. Art auctions can be unpredictable. In late 2011, Bonhams Auctions in New York re-offered the 25"x30" (two-sided) painting with a $40-$60,000 estimate. Once again it did not sell for the minimum bid.

Six Degrees Of Separation: Art Just Around 6 Corners!

"Six Degrees of Separation" is the idea that everyone in the world is connected to everyone else by a chain of no more than six acquaintances. If that's true, then you could be only six people away from finding a Van Gogh or a Picasso! The truth is, there are millions of valuable paintings "just around the corner" - or perhaps six corners! Some may be worth $100. Some may be worth a fortune. If you are willing to sort through the trash to get to the treasure, it's out there waiting for you.

In the next chapter, we will teach you how to appraise valuable art. "The Four Aces Of Art Hunting" represent an indispensable tool that you'll need to hunt down and capture a painting that may be worth the price of a new car. Like a lottery ticket, this book could change your life. Sure, very few people will find a painting for $5 that's worth $1,000,000. However, in our "Artist Profile" chapter, we will introduce you to 120 valuable artists whose art does not always "look valuable." As an art hunter, you may very well encounter one or more of these artists. And remember, there are 240,000 artists whose work can be researched. In our opinon, it's "likely" that you can find several valuable paintings a year at garage sales and flea markets. To pursue the "six degrees of separation" concept seriously, print up some "We Buy Oil Paintings" cards to hand out to friends, and to post in laundromats and supermarkets. Run ads on Craigslist and scour eBay. And tell everyone you know you'd like to buy old paintings. There is no doubt that you're going to make some cool connections and some fabulous finds.

Think Of The Art Hunters Handbook As A Lottery Ticket. With Better Odds.

Untitled Coastal Scene – 12" x 16" Oil on Board
Rago Art & Auctions $7,800 (9/13/08)

Cornella Thompson Farm – 9" x 10" Oil on Canvasboard
Freeman's Auctioneers $11,880 (12/6/09)

Houses In The Snow – 14" x 16" Oil on Canvas
Freeman's Auctioneers $12,500 (12/7/08)

Harbor Scene – 10" x 12" Oil on Canvasboard
Christie's $14,400 (3/9/07)

Fern I. Coppedge.

FERN I. COPPEDGE   American (1883-1951)

Fern Coppedge, the only woman artist in Pennsylvania's "New Hope" school, was born in Decatur, Illinois. A talented Impressionist, Coppedge's unique style and colors have been compared to Fauvists and Post-Impressionists. Interestingly, no drawings, sketches or watercolors by this artist have been sold at auction. Her record price is over $300,000 (see Artist Profile pages) but dozens of her paintings turn up every year. If you're lucky enough to find one, and you just might, her average oil painting is worth at least $5,000 to $10,000. There are many fake Coppedges on the market so please read our chapter on Appraisals and Authentication. Free advice and appraisals are available from art experts Les and Sue Fox / West Highland Art Auction Brokers at www.AmericanArtAdvisor.com.

MOST LIKELY ARTISTS TO FIND

AT GARAGE SALES, FLEA MARKETS, ESTATE SALES, CONSIGNMENT SHOPS & AUCTIONS

Village Scape – 10" x 13" Pencil on Paper
Outer Cape Auctions $633 (2/18/07)

A Summer Day, 1927 – 12" x 16" Oil on Board
Alderfer Auctions $805 (9/12/08)

Still Life With Fruit – 10" x 13" Oil on Masonite
James Julia Auctions $1,092 (8/27/04)

Bass Rocks – 12" x 16" Oil on Canvasboard
Bonhams San Francisco $1,380 (12/8/98)

Emile A Gruppe

EMILE GRUPPE   American (1896-1978)

Born in Rochester, New York, Emile Gruppe was a prolific New England landscape and marine Impressionist. He painted tirelessly in his Gloucester, Massachusetts studio. Emile Gruppe probably created more than 10,000 canvases during his lifetime, as well as a large number of drawings and sketches. In addition to his finest work, which can bring up to $60,000 (see Artist Profile pages), people often discover Gruppes worth $500 to $2,500. If you have a sharp eye, you are likely to find one or more Gruppes in your travels.

OTHER ARTISTS TO LOOK FOR: Hayley Lever, Anthony Thieme, Aldro Hibbard, Rolph Scarlett, David Burliuk, Johann Berthelsen, Edouard Cortes. (Note: A painting titled *Art Critics* by Joseph Decker, the artist on the front cover, has been missing for many years.)

BUYING TIPS: Don't discuss auction prices when you're buying a painting. Make sure it's an original, not a print. And always get a bill of sale, especially if you pay cash.

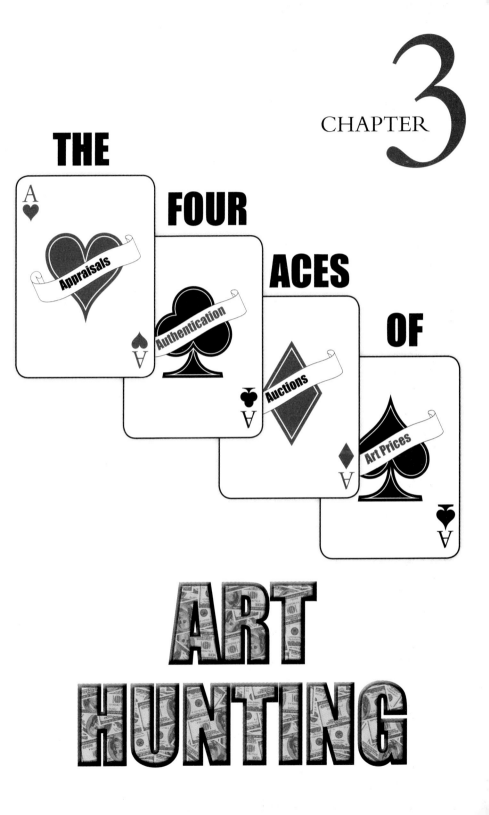

True or False? "The value of art is based mainly on its beauty." The answer is: False. The value of art is based mainly on the fame of the artist. Yes, it's true that most people consider Claude Monet's landscapes, lily ponds and flower gardens "beautiful" as well as valuable. But it's also true that paintings of large rectangles by Mark Rothko, whether considered beautiful or not, are worth up to $70 million. While at the same time, "beautiful" landscapes by less famous artists like Fern Coppedge and Hayley Lever are worth only a fraction of the value. *(See Artist Profile pages.)*

So how does one appraise a painting based on the fame of an artist? Is there a mathematical formula to convert fame to dollars? Actually there is: Public auction records. The 240,000 artists on AskART are not ranked according to fame, but fame is automatically reflected by each artist's price levels. *Higher auction prices = More fame.* If you review their auctions, you will see that Monet and Rothko consistently sell for millions of dollars. Coppedge and Lever, on the other hand, sell for $10,000 to $100,000. Therefore, the two higher priced artists are 100 to 1,000 times as famous (and as valuable) as the other two. Remember: Beauty is in the eye of the beholder, but auction prices are cold, hard facts.

Thanks to the information available online, you can now access millions of auction results - including pre-sale estimates, prices realized and photos of most of the actual paintings sold - for a very modest fee. Ten or fifteen years ago, you needed a vast, expensive library to research auctions, and it took infinitely longer to look up paintings. By comparing prices, images and sizes online, you can quickly get a general idea of how much a painting is worth. Important factors like subject, condition and provenance affect market value. If an artist is not listed online, you may not be able to do further research.

APPRAISALS: HOW WE IDENTIFY "ORIGINAL" PAINTINGS

We receive thousands of inquiries a year from people who think they've found an original painting which turns out to be a reproduction. Don't be discouraged if that $10 million "Picasso" is really a $10 print. Most Picassos are in museums and billionaire art collections. Your job is to identify and evaluate original paintings. This book is not about finding Picassos. It's about developing an "eye" for paintings worth at least $1,000 to $10,000, and then determining fair market value through public auction records.

Step 1: Recognizing Reproductions. An original oil painting exhibits the following characteristics:

(1) ***You can see and feel the paint.*** Oil paint has texture. It displays a "raised" appearance, including visible brushstrokes. (Warning: "Giclees" imitate original oil paintings.) There is no harm in gently touching the surface of a painting to feel the paint. If the back of your painting is covered, feel free to carefully remove the paper. As long as you don't cut the canvas, this will not detract from the value.

(2) ***The canvas is nailed to a wooden stretcher.*** A "stretcher" is the "inner frame" which holds the painted canvas tightly in place. From the 19th Century (and earlier) until at least the 1950's artists hammered nails along the "tacking edge" of oil paintings. During the second half of the 20th century, people began using staples (as well as nails) to attach the canvases. If your painting is stapled to the stretcher, it may be not be as old as you think. But it could still be a winner.

(3) ***A painting "shows its age."*** Just like people, cars and houses, old paintings look old. Wood darkens to yellow or brown. Spots and stains appear on the back of the canvas, as well as on the stretcher and the frame. Joints loosen and separate as old glue dries out and the wood shrinks. The paint also dries and cracks. (Which often can be restored.) So if your "antique" painting looks fresh and new, most likely it was recently painted. Or it's a reproduction. (Caution: Some forgers re-use the canvas of an antique painting to disguise the age of a fake.)

(4) ***Watercolors.*** Unlike oil paintings, watercolors are flat and do not exhibit raised paint. Learn to recognize the thickness and texture of watercolor paper. If you remove a watercolor painting from its matte, or border, you'll see that the actual painted area is larger than the rectangular, viewable portion of the design. Watercolors

are not painted as perfect rectangles. If the edge of your artwork is a perfect rectangle, it's probably a print. Again, there is no harm in removing a watercolor from its housing as long as you don't damage the painting.

Signs Of A Reproduction. Paper labels. Metal plates. Printed museum or gallery descriptions. Serial numbers. And pencil signatures. What we usually tell people if they're uncertain about whether they own an original is to ask a local art gallery or frame shop. You can also bring it to a museum or art school. As mentioned above, "giclees" can be deceptive. That's because they are "computer generated" reproductions designed to look like original oil paintings. Sometimes they are "highlighted" with real paint, such as Thomas Kinkade's decorative art prints. As a rule, post-1940 prints, lithographs, serigraphs and signed limited editions are worth very little compared to originals.

"Paintings" by the following artists almost always turn out to be prints or fakes: Grandma Moses, Andy Warhol, Pablo Picasso, Norman Rockwell, Salvador Dali, Andrew Wyeth, Mark Chagall, Albert Bierstadt, Edward Potthast, Jane Peterson, Guy Wiggins, and most other famous artists. Below (left) is a photo of the original *Still Life With Apples And Oranges* by Paul Cezanne (worth millions) along with a "possible Cezanne" that was sent to us by a private party who hoped he'd discovered a genuine "alternative version" of the same painting. The owner did not have any documentation (letters, exhibition labels or invoices). We advised letting us guide him through the process of determining if this is an old *copy* of a Cezanne but we have not heard from him again. Added signatures and other

alterations to paintings can be easily detected with a "black light" (ultra-violet). When viewed in a dark room under ultra-violet light, changes to the original surface of a painting show up in shades of

purple, a dead giveaway that a painting has been changed.

Halfway House by the American Impressionist Hugh Bolton Jones is a very interesting example of a popular reproduction. At least a few people a month contact us about the value of this "painting." As it turns out, not only is *Halfway House* a print. It's actually a "fantasy concept", dated 1876, created for S&H Green Stamps in the 1970's as a catalog promotion! That's right. According to Jones expert Joan Ziebel and various museums we contacted, Hugh Bolton Jones never painted this landscape! The scene is reminiscent of the artist's style. But the ducks in the pond, the covered wagon and the boaters are simply designed to make the painting look interesting. In fact, the historic "Halfway House" was actually in Brooklyn, New York, and was not surrounded by water or mountains. The mass produced print was published by Windsor Art Products of Los Angeles. We'd love to know who painted the original of the (non- original) *Halfway House*, but our research has failed to turn up the talented 1970's artist. By the way, the signature doesn't match Jones' real signature either. (Examples of many artists' signature styles are available online.)

ART AUTHENTICATION

Just because a painting is signed "Picasso" doesn't mean that's who painted it. It's easy to forge a Picasso signature, and it's not difficult for a decent artist to create a nice "tribute" to the Master. Yet people regularly buy fake Picassos online and at flea markets for hundreds of dollars thinking they bought a painting (or drawing) of great value. Some sellers are innocent, but others concoct elaborate schemes, including fake letters of authentication, fake ownership

Fake Museum Label

history, fake private estate sales, and fake museum labels. The odds of "finding" a genuine Picasso are miniscule, other than commercial "limited editions" or art thefts. If you think you've found the real McCoy, show it to a local art gallery.

If they think your Picasso might be real, the next step is to submit it to an auction house, or to the authors of this book. Experts follow a careful process of authentication, which includes visual comparison with known genuine works, invoices, letters, exhibition or auction records, provenance (most

Fake Picasso

Picassos can be traced back to the original owner) and occasionally forensic analysis. Written authentication can involve considerable expense. An expert opinion will provide a starting point for further research.

The "painting" below by William Merritt Chase dated 1904 ('04) was offered to us in its original antique frame with the name of Chase's 19th century dealers (Duran & Devilder, Paris), stamped on the back of the canvas board. Unfortunately, this work of art is a high quality antique print.

ART AUCTIONS: HOW TO RESEARCH ART PRICES

More than 120,000 paintings are sold at public auction every year. These auctions will join the millions of past auction records listed online, including photos, sizes and the name of the auction house. When you find a painting that may be valuable, just look

up the artist's name. If an artist is not listed, you may have to dig further. For every artist with an auction track record, there are hundreds of talented artists, especially living artists, who do not enjoy a "resale market" at auction. This is not to say that your uncle's masterpieces, or the work of a contemporary artist, are of little value. Some living artists are sold only in private art galleries, and often for high prices. We are simply informing you that as an Art Hunter, the easiest paintings to appraise for potential

Note lack of brushstrokes on Anthony Thieme print. Most original oil paintings do not exhibit uniform texture.

profit are those done by "listed" artists with public auction records. A listed artist's biography includes important art schools attended, famous art instructors, gallery and museum exhibitions, book references and being included in serious art collections. If you can't read an artist's name from the signature, unfortunately that may be a dead end. However, many art dealers will try to help you figure out who the artist is.

Next, let's take a look at a fascinating modern artist named Conrad Marca-relli who once lived in Wayne, New Jersey. Marca-relli was a friend and contemporary of Jackson Pollock. One of his paintings was auctioned for over $1,000,000. Studying Conrad Marca-relli illustrates how to systematically analyze and appraise paintings of any time period. On November 9, 2011 two similar oil paintings / collages by Conrad Marca-relli (below) were sold at

Summer Rain. 59" x 77" $56,250

The Expendible. 32" x 53" $146,500

Christie's in New York. The black, white and gold painting brought $56,250. The black and white painting brought $146,500. Why? Clearly, the painting on the left is larger, more colorful and more interesting. So it should be more valuable, right? Wrong. Remember, the market value of art is not about beauty, it's about fame. Just as Marca-relli is more famous (and valuable) than thousands of abstract expressionists, his earlier work is more valuable than his later work. The painting on the left was created in 1986. The more expensive one was created in 1957 when Marca-relli and Pollock were working at the same time. Regardless of whether you might personally prefer *Summer Rain* to *The Expendible*, Marca-relli's "period" painting was done when the artist was at the peak of his creativity and popularity. Auction records of this groundbreaking modernist can be perplexing. For example, Marca-relli's record price was set in 2006 when Christie's sold his panoramic masterpiece *St. Cyprian's Day* for $441,600. Then guess what ? Christie's *re-auctioned* the monumental 55" x 136" painting in 2008 with a pre-sale estimate of $400-$600,000. The painting sold only two years later for a whopping $1,105,000, defying the popular theory that the same painting cannot be successfully auctioned more than once every 10 years. In this book we try to set down useful rules for you to follow, but you need to think outside the box.

St. Cyprian's Day. (1957–58) $441,600 or $1,105,000?

GUY WIGGINS: NEW YORK SNOW SCENES

As American art buffs know, Guy Carleton Wiggins (1883-1962) was the most successful painter of 19th and 20th century New York City winter cityscapes. Criticized for his repetitiveness (Wiggins painted thousands of similar views), the fact remains that this Connecticut impressionist's distinctive visions of Fifth Avenue and Wall Street "cloaked in white" inspire competitive bidding at public auction. For more than a decade, Wiggins' winter scenes have sold for $50,000 to $150,000 or more. Following his record price of $374,000 for a 28" x 42" canvas of the New York Stock Exchange in 2005, prices retreated a bit. Like the stock market, the art market can be very volatile. Prices can go down as well as up. Yet, as shown below, a prominent American flag could add $100,000 to the value of a great Wiggins! Yellow and green buses and taxi cabs, architectural details, and the number of colorful pedestrians fighting their way through the snow also factor into the desirability and price of a Guy Wiggins. In studying more than 750 auctions by Wiggins online, it's challenging to figure out exactly what makes one Wiggins worth more than another. Note: Collectors of Guy Wiggins' summer landscapes and harbor scenes often get a bargain compared to his more popular winter scenes. Warning: There are many fake Wiggins' on the market, including paintings with fake gallery labels, fake hand-written inscriptions and fake invoices. For years, Guy Wiggins' son (born in 1920 and also named Guy) authenticated his father's paintings. Guy A. Wiggins also painted New York City winter scenes which have sold at auction for up to $40,000. Another artist who painted New York City winter scenes was Wiggins' contemporary, Johann Berthelsen.

Christie's 2007
(24"x20") $300,000

Sotheby's 2006
(16"x12") $180,000

Christie's 2010
(16"x12") $158,500

Sotheby's 2006
(24"x20") $96,000

Sotheby's 2006
(24"x20") $84,000

Christie's 2004
(20"x16") $74,000

FOUR ACES: A WINNING HAND

Using AskART's auction price database to compare and evaluate paintings is an art as well as a science. Plus, it's an indispensable tool to the serious Art Hunter who needs to know how much to pay for a genuine work of art. Auction results can be easily sorted by auction date, price, size, media, subject matter and auction house. You can compare the pre-sale estimate to the actual price realized. (Keep in mind that final prices generally include a 20% buyer's fee.) Auction records also include paintings that failed to meet the "reserve" (or minimum bid), which is based on the low estimate. You will occasionally see that a painting was offered for sale more than once within several years. It can be the kiss of death when a painting fails to sell at public auction. Regardless of the reason (usually too high an estimate), collectors typically assume there was something wrong with "re-auctioned" paintings, like "Olive Trees" by Frederick Frieseke in Chapter 2. One last comment about auctions, other than the recommendation to learn all you can: The stock market can affect auction prices. Even though Wall Street technically has nothing to do with the art market, if the stock market is having a bad week art collectors may not be in a good buying mood. Whereas, if stocks are up, an art auction may do better than expected!

"Doing your homework" is sometimes as simple as determining that an artist was famous for landscapes and not portraits. From that point, comparing landscapes of similar size and subject matter (by the same artist) will help you understand why one painting sold for $25,000 and another for $50,000. As each artist's auction prices rise, you will see a pattern. There is no "simple formula" or exact science for accurately appraising every painting. Don't be afraid to ask art dealers, art experts and auction houses for their professional opinions. Most dealers will be happy to answer your questions. The more you study this chapter and our Artist Profile pages, the better you will understand art auctions. Hopefully, you will be fascinated, and stimulated to learn more. There are big rewards for Art Hunters with the ambition to learn about the art auction market.

4 ACES

ART HUNTER TIPS

Never assume that a painting isn't worth much just because you don't like it.

The value of art may have little to do with what you personally consider "beautiful." Also, a larger painting is not automatically more valuable than a smaller painting. Comparing auction prices is, in our opinion, the best way to determine value.

The "Prices Realized" or "Sold At Auction" prices reported throughout this book usually include a 20% "buyer's fee", which is over and above the "hammer" price.

When a painting is "sold" at auction, the "hammer price" is the final bid. However, the auction house then charges an additional "Buyer's Fee", usually 20%. So a painting "sold" for $12,000 often represents a hammer price of $10,000 plus a Buyer's Fee of $2,000.

Authenticity and Provenance.

Unless a painting is unquestionably genuine, it will be hard to sell in a reputable auction. Experts decide if a painting is genuine. Authenticity is based on recognizing the work of the artist and the provenance or known history of the painting. Often, the age of the canvas, stretcher and frame help determine authenticity, as do invoices, art gallery and exhibition labels.

"Fresh To The Market" Sells.

Collectors are excited to bid at auction on paintings that have not been on the market for at least 10 or 20 years. A painting which was sold at auction in the past few years will generally bring less money when it is re-sold.

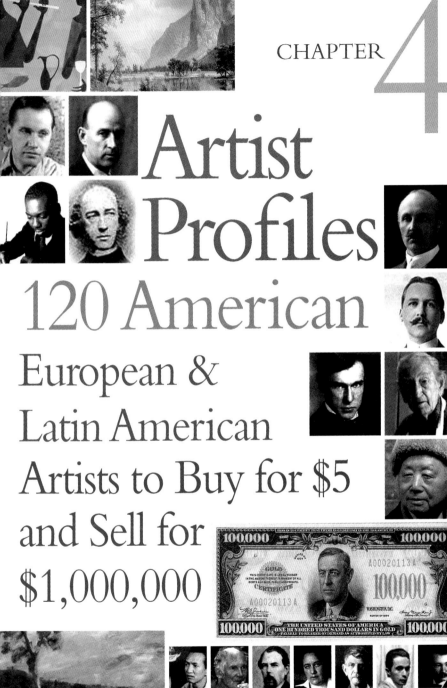

CHAPTER 4

Artist Profiles

120 American European & Latin American Artists to Buy for $5 and Sell for $1,000,000

I f you want to be a serious Art Hunter, you've come to the right place. The *Artist Profile* pages ahead will acquaint you with a diverse group of 19th and 20th century artists from Hudson River School to Impressionism, Cubism, Modernism and Abstract art. Some artists are worth only a few thousand dollars, but many are worth *millions*. Can you tell which are which? Take a test! Turn to a random page and put your hand over everything except the painting. Then try to guess the auction price. You may be surprised, even stunned, at some of the prices. Repeat this test with paintings you like and don't like. Proof that the value of art is based on fame and auction prices.

Man Crazy Nurse
by Richard Prince
($7,433,000)

VS

Winter Landscape
by George Gardner
Symons ($130,000)

For example, *Man Crazy Nurse* by Richard Prince (born in 1949) was sold at auction in 2008 for $7,433,000, while *Winter Landscape* by George Gardner Symons (1863-1930) was sold in 2007 for the artist's record price of only $130,000. Being able to place an accurate market value on any

painting will give you the Art Hunter's edge, and the key to profit.

Our Artist Profile pages feature a signature, a biography, the artist's style and a general price range. (Important: The "Prices

Realized" or "Sold At Auction" prices generally include a 20% "buyer's fee", over and above the "hammer" price.) Plus, we recommend three museums where you can view their work to compare brushstrokes, size, subject matter and colors and become knowledgeable about specific artists. You can also "visit" these artists on the internet via AskART, Google and Wikipedia.

In the art world, we have met many "pickers." A picker is actually an *Art Hunter*. Some of the best pickers are self-taught, average people *without* art degrees or years of experience in an art gallery. Highly motivated to track down valuable paintings, pickers have a single goal in mind: Finding good art. They tirelessly visit garage sales and flea markets, estate sales and auctions, eBay, Goodwill, the Salvation Army, antique shops and jewelry stores, looking behind furniture, moving cartons aside, taking paintings off walls to see if there is documentation on the back, and making deals.

Perseverance is the key. A picker will happily spend the day to buy a painting for $5 (or $500) to sell to a dealer or auction broker for a profit. Because he or she knows that *the million-dollar payday* may be only one pick away! The serious Art Hunter will go anywhere for a find. He will ask friends, relatives, even complete strangers if they know who has art for sale. He can and will find it, and buy it for the right price. And so can you!

In 1968, the year we were married, Les and Sue Fox realized that art hunting is in our blood. On our honeymoon we attended art auctions and began the learning process. We've done our homework, and we've been avid art collectors and art brokers for over 40 years. We love to hunt for paintings! We sincerely hope that after reading *The Art Hunters Handbook* you will, too. Happy hunting!

JOSEF ALBERS

Albers

German / American (1888–1976)

HOMAGE TO THE SQUARE: JOY

Sold At Auction 11/14/07
$1,497,000
Sotheby's New York

Oil On Masonite
Size: 48" x 48"

Price Range:
$35,000 to $1,500,000

Biography: Born in Bottrop, Germany. Emigrated to North Carolina 1933. Geometric Abstractionist.
Museums: Solomon Guggenheim, Metropolitan Museum Of Art, Hirschhorn Museum And Sculpture Garden

MILTON AVERY

Milton Avery

American (1885–1965)

THE READER AND THE LISTENER

Sold At Auction 11/28/07
$2,505,000
Sotheby's New York

Oil On Canvas
Size: 30" x 40"

Price Range:
$5,000 to $2,500,000

Biography: Born in Altmar, New York. Modernist. (Self-taught.)
Museums: Metropolitan Museum Of Art, Chrysler Museum, National Gallery Of Art

Free Art Appraisals – Please Visit: www.AmericanArtAdvisor.com

DANA BARTLETT

DANA BARTLETT

American (1882-1957)

BY THE SEA

Sold At Auction 6/19/02
$77,680
Christie's Los Angeles

Oil On Canvas
Size: 40" x 49"

Price Range:
$2,000 to $80,000

Biography: Born in Ionia, Michigan. California Impressionist.
Museums: Irvine Museum, Laguna Beach Museum Of Art

WILL BARNET

Will Barnet

American (1911-)

YOUNG WOMAN WITH CAT

Sold At Auction 9/30/09
$25,000
Sotheby's New York

Gouache and Pencil on Paper / Board
Size: 28" x 25"

Price Range:
$4,000 to $50,000

Biography: Born in Beverly, Massachusetts. Abstract Expressionist, Stylized Realist (Portraits)
Museums: Boston Museum Of Fine Arts, Whitney Museum, Pennsylvania Academy Of Fine Arts

WALTER EMERSON BAUM

W.E. BAUM

American (1884-1956)

From The Authors Collection

PENNSYLVANIA HILLS, WINTER

Sold At Auction 6/27/04
$58,750
Freeman's Auctioneers

Oil On Canvas
Size: 30" x 36"

Price Range:
$5,000 to $100,000

Biography: Born in Sellersville, PA. Pennsylvania Impressionist.
Museums: Michener Art Museum, Pennsylvania Academy Of Fine Arts, Butler Institute

ROBERT ALAN BECHTLE

RB

American (1932-)

Photo Copyright Artist Or Assignee.

S.F. CADILLAC

Sold At Auction 5/12/10
$482,500
Christie's New York

Oil On Canvas
Size: 41" x 59"

Price Range:
$7,500 to $500,000

Biography: Born in San Francisco, CA. Photo Realist.
Museums: San Francisco Museum Of Modern Art, Crocker Art Museum, Guggenheim

THOMAS HART BENTON
American (1889-1975)

POLITICS, FARMING AND LAW IN MISSOURI

Sold At Auction 12/03/03
$355,200
Sotheby's New York

Mixed Media / Board
Size: 18" x 28"

Price Range:
$3,500 to $2,500,000

Biography: Born in Neosho, Missouri. Modernist / Realist / Regionalist.
Museums: Carnegie Museum Of Pittsburgh, Corcoran Gallery, Metropolitan Museum

CUNDO BERMUDEZ
Cuban (1914-2008)

PAREJA EN LA MESA

Sold At Auction 5/26/11
$206,500
Christies New York

Oil On Canvas
Size: 40" x 50"

Price Range:
$10,000 to $200,000

Biography: Born in La Habana, Cuba. Emigrated to U.S. in 1967. Modernist.
Museums: Museum Of Modern Art, Lowe Art Museum.

Free Art Appraisals – Please Visit: www.AmericanArtAdvisor.com

JOHANN BERTHELSEN

Johann Berthelson

American (1883-1972)

THE GREEN BUS, FIFTH AVENUE

Sold At Auction 5/4/06
$31,070
Shannon's Auctioneers

Oil On Canvas
Size: 20" x 24"

Price Range:
$2,500 to $45,000

Biography: Born in Copenhagen, Denmark. Emigrated to New York 1890. Impressionist.
Museums: Butler Institute, Panhandle-Plain Historical Museum, Sheldon Swope Art Museum

ALBERT BIERSTADT

Bierstadt

American (1830-1902)

YOSEMITE VALLEY

Sold At Auction 12/3/03
$7,176,000
Sotheby's New York

Oil On Canvas
Size: 39" x 61"

Price Range:
$10,000 to $7,500,000

Biography: Born in Solingen, Germany. Emigrated to New York circa 1830. Hudson River School Landscapes.
Museums: Smithsonian, Metropolitan Museum, National Gallery Of Art

Free Art Appraisals – Please Visit: www.AmericanArtAdvisor.com

ELMER BISCHOFF

E B

American (1916-1991)

RED CLIFFS

Sold At Auction 5/10/06
$564,800
Christie's New York

Oil On Canvas
Size: 78" x 103"

Price Range:
$2,500 to $550,000

Biography: Born in Berkeley, Ca. Abstract Expressionist / Figures.
Museums: Crocker Art Museum, San Francisco Museum of Modern Art, Yale Univ. Art Gallery

FRANZ BISCHOFF

Franz A Bischoff

American (1864-1929)

ROSES

Sold At Auction 8/3/09
$798,000
Bonhams San Francisco

Oil On Canvas
Size: 40" x 50"

Price Range:
$2,500 to $800,000

Biography: Born in Bomen, Austria. Emigrated to N.Y. City 1885, Los Angeles 1900. California. Impressionist/Roses.
Museums: Chrysler Museum, San Diego Museum of Art, Irvine Museum

LAVERNE NELSON BLACK

LaVerne Nelson Black

American (1887-1938)

FIESTA TIME AT TAOS

Sold At Auction 5/24/06
$531,200
Sotheby's New York

Oil On Canvas
Size: 30" x 36"

Price Range:
$2,500 to $550,000

Biography: Born in Viola, Wisconsin. Impressionist / Western Genre
Museums: Phoenix Art Museum, Smithsonian, Stark Museum Of Art

ANTOINE BLANCHARD

Antoine. Blanchard.

American (1910-1988)

A VIEW OF THE THEATRE DU VAUDEVILLE

Sold At Auction 5/16/07
$24,000
Bonhams San Francisco

Oil On Canvas
Size: 18" x 22"

Price Range:
$4,000 to $25,000

Biography: Born in Loire Valley, France. Impressionist / 1890's Paris Scenes.
Museums: (None) Reference: "Antoine Blanchard: His Life, His Work" by A.P. Lardet

Free Art Appraisals - Please Visit: www.AmericanArtAdvisor.com

OSCAR BLUEMNER

Ꝋ⅃ᙏ⅃Ꝋ

American (1867–1938)

Photo Copyright Artist Or Assignee.

ILLUSION OF A PRAIRIE, NEW JERSEY

Sold At Auction 11/30/11
$5,346,500
Christies New York

Oil On Canvas
Size: 30" x 40"

Price Range:
$2,500 to $5,500,000

Biography: Born in Germany. Emigrated to New York. Cubist / Futurist.
Museums: Amon Carter Museum, Museum Of Fine Arts Boston, Newark Museum

ALIGHIERO BOETTI

AL I G

Italian (1940–1994)

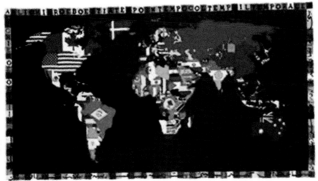

Photo Copyright Artist Or Assignee.

MAPPA

Sold At Auction 6/30/10
$2,762,520
Christie's London

Embroidered Tapestry
Size: 46" x 85"

Price Range:
$5,000 to $2,750,000

Biography: Born in Turin, Italy. Conceptualist / Mixed Media (Embroidered Maps)
Museums: Museum Of Modern Art

Free Art Appraisals – Please Visit: www.AmericanArtAdvisor.com

JESSE ARMS BOTKE

JESSIE ARMS BOTKE

American (1883–1971)

COCKATOOS AND AVOCADO

Sold At Auction 10/24/07
$85,000
Christie's Los Angeles

Oil On Canvas
Size: 25" x 30"

Price Range:
$1,500 to $90,000

Biography: Born in Chicago. Moved to California. Realist / Naturalist (Exotic Birds)
Museums: Art Institute of Chicago, National Museum Of Wildlife Art, San Diego Museum Of Art

MAURICE BRAUN

Maurice Braun

American (1877–1941)

THE BAY – SAN DIEGO

Sold At Auction 6/25/98
$145,000
Bonhams San Francisco

Oil On Canvas
Size: 34" x 34"

Price Range:
$4,000 to $180,000

Biography: Born in Nagy Bittse, Hungary. Emigrated to N.Y. City. Settled in California. California Impressionist.
Museums: Museum Of Fine Arts Houston, San Diego Museum Of Art, Museum Of Art At Brigham Young University

GLENN BROWN

British (1966-)

FILTH, 2004

Sold At Auction 5/12/11
$2,546,500
Phillips, dePury & Co

Oil On Panel
Size: 52" x 37"

Price Range:
$200,000 to $2,500,000

Photo Copyright Artist Or Assignee.

Biography: Born in Northumberland, England. Surrealist.
Museums: (None) Exhibition Museum Of Contemporary Arts, Los Angeles (2005)

CONRAD BUFF

American (1886–1975)

CANYON LAND

Sold At Auction 11/18/03
$77,000
John Moran Auctioneers

Oil On Masonite
Size: 34" x 51"

Price Range:
$1,500 to $75,000

Photo Copyright Artist Or Assignee.

Biography: Born in Speicher, Switzerland. Emigrated to Los Angeles in 1907. Modernist (Landscapes)
Museums: Los Angeles County Museum Of Art, Phoenix Art Museum, San Diego Museum Of Art

CHARLES E. BURCHFIELD

Charles E. Burchfield

American (1883-1967)

A DREAM OF BUTTERFLIES

Sold At Auction 11/28/07
$1,329,000
Sotheby's New York

Watercolor / Paper
Size: 33" x 39"

Price Range:
$5,000 to $1,300,000

Biography: Born in Ashtabula, Ohio. Moved to Buffalo. Modernist / Botanical
Museums: Burchfield / Penny Art Center Buffalo, Metropolitan Museum Of Art, National Gallery Of Art

DAVID BURLIUK

BURLIUK.

Russian - American (1882-1967)

PEASANT WITH CHICKENS, 1953

Sold At Auction 4/7/10
$92,500
Phillips de Pury & Co.

Oil On Canvas
Size: 26" x 40"

Price Range:
$2,500 to $700,000

Biography: Born in Kharkov, Ukraine. Emigrated to New York 1922. Modernist (Still Lifes / Figures)
Museums: Brooklyn Museum Of Art, Heckscher Museum, Whitney Museum

Free Art Appraisals - Please Visit: www.AmericanArtAdvisor.com

CHEN CHI

Chinese (1912-2005)

LOTUS AND LITTLE FISH

Sold At Auction 12/15/07
$28,200
Altermann Galleries

Watercolor/Paper
Size: 32" x 59"

Price Range:
$1,000 to $36,000

Biography: Born in Wu-sih, Kiangsu, China. Lived in New York. Modernist (Landscape/Urban Imagery)
Museums: Butler Institute of American Art, The Columbus Museum, Georgia

ANTONIO CIRINO

American (1889-1983)

FOR SALE

Sold At Auction 4/28/05
$18,800
Shannon's Auctioneers

Oil On Canvas
Size: 25" x 30"

Price Range:
$1,000 to $19,000

Biography: Born in Italy. Emigrated to the U.S. in 1892.1920's Settled in Rhode Island. Impressionist (Landscape/Coastal)
Museums: Salmagundi Museum of American Art

ALSON SKINNER CLARK

Alson Clark

American (1876-1949)

BRIDGE BUILDERS

Sold At Auction 8/7/07
$204,000
Bonhams San Francisco

Oil On Canvas
Size: 30" x 38"

Price Range:
$2,000 to $200,000

Photo Copyright Artist Or Assignee.

Biography: Born in Chicago. Moved to California 1919. California Impressionist.
Museums: Art Institute of Chicago, Greenville County Museum of Art, San Diego Museum of Art

COLIN CAMPBELL COOPER

Colin Campbell Cooper

American (1856-1937)

NEW YORK PUBLIC LIBRARY

Sold At Auction 5/21/08
$881,000
Christie's New York

Oil On Canvas
Size: 29" x 36"

Price Range:
$5,000 to $880,000

Photo Copyright Artist Or Assignee.

Biography: Born in Philadelphia. Settled in California 1921. California/New York Impressionist (City, Portraits)
Museums: Cincinnati Art Museum, San Diego Museum of Art, Brooklyn Museum, The White House

Free Art Appraisals - Please Visit: www.AmericanArtAdvisor.com

FERN I. COPPEDGE

Fern I Coppedge.

American (1883–1951)

THE DELAWARE VALLEY

Sold At Auction 12/3/06
$308,030
Freeman's Auctioneers

Oil On Canvas
Size: 38" x 40"

Price Range:
$6,000 to $300,000

Photo Copyright Artist Or Assignee.

Biography: Born Decatur, IL. Moved New Hope PA 1920. PA Impressionist.
Museums: Bryn Mawr College, Michener Art Museum, Reading Public Museum

EDOUARD LEON CORTES

Edouard Cortes.

French (1882–1969)

BOULEVARD SAINT MARTIN

Sold At Auction 12/12/11
$43,920
Leslie Hindman
Auctioneers

Oil On Canvas
Size: 18" x 22"

Price Range:
$8,000 to $115,000

Photo Copyright Artist Or Assignee.

Biography: Born Lagny, France. Impressionist (Paris Street Scenes).
Museums: (None) Studied at Ecole des Beaux-Arts in Paris. First Exhibition 1899

Free Art Appraisals – Please Visit: www.AmericanArtAdvisor.com

JOHN COSTIGAN

V. E. Costigan

American (1888–1972)

Photo Copyright Artist Or Assignee.

SHEEP AT THE BROOK

Sold At Auction 9/27/11
$43,750
Christie's New York

Oil On Canvas
Size: 34" x 40"

Price Range:
$3,500 to $45,000

Biography: Born Providence, R.I. Moved to NY. Self Taught Impressionist. (Pastoral)
Museums: Smithsonian, Butler Museum Of Art, Brooklyn Museum Of Art

EANGER IRVING COUSE

E.I. COUSE - N.A.

American (1866–1936)

Photo Copyright Artist Or Assignee.

THE LESSON

Sold At Auction 5/20/98
$618,500
Sotheby's New York

Oil On Canvas
Size: 50" x 60"

Price Range:
$5,000 to $950,000

Biography: Born Saginaw, MI. Moved Taos, NM 1927. (Western/Native American.)
Museums: Albuquerque Museum, Arizona Art Museum, Smithsonian

ROBERT CRUMB

R. CRUMB

American (1943-)

MR. NATURAL #1 COVER

Sold At Auction 11/17/07
$101,580
Heritage Auctions

Ink & Zipatone/Paper
Size: 10" x 14"

Price Range:
$1,000 to $100,000

Biography: Born in Phila., PA. 1980's Lived in Ca. 1990's settled in France. Cartoonist (Funk/Fantasy.)
Museums: Cartoon Art Museum

ALLAN D'ARCANGELO

D'ARCANGELO

American (1930-1998)

Art © Estate of Allan M. D'Arcangelo/Licensed by VAGA, New York, NY

U.S. HIGHWAY 1, NO. 4

Sold At Auction 5/15/08
$802,600
Sotheby's New York

Oil On Canvas
Size: 71" x 81"

Price Range:
$5,000 to $800,000

Biography: Born Buffalo, NY. Pop Art/Modernist
Museums: Butler Institute of American Art, Dallas Museum of Art, Whitney

JOSEPH DECKER

J. Decker

American (1853–1924)

THE RED ADMIRAL

Sold At Auction 11/30/89
$759,000
Sotheby's New York

Oil On Canvas
Size: 8" x 14"

Price Range:
$7,500 to $760,000

Biography: Born Wurttemburg, Germany. 1867 settled in New York. Realist/Impressionist (Still Life.)
Museums: National Gallery of Art, PA Academy of Fine Arts, Yale University Art Gallery

STUART DAVIS

Stuart Davis

American (1892–1964)

Art © Estate of Stuart Davis/Licensed by VAGA, New York, NY

ARCADE

Sold At Auction 12/1/10
$362,500
Christie's New York

Oil On Canvas
Size: 12" x 16"

Price Range:
$10,000 to $4,500,000

Biography: Born Phila., PA. Moved to New York City. Cubist/Abstract Modernist
Museums: Metropolitan Museum, National Gallery Of Art, Museum Of Modern Art

ANDRE DERAIN

French (1880-1954)

ARBRES A COLLIOURE

Sold At Auction 6/22/10
$23,962,740
Sotheby's London

Oil On Canvas
Size: 26" x 32"

Price Range:
$3,000 to $24,000,000

Biography: Born Chatou, France. Fauvist/Pointillist
Museums: Museum of Modern Art, National Gallery of Art, Brooklyn Museum

MAYNARD DIXON

American (1875-1946)

STORY TELLERS

Sold At Auction 7/30/05
$1,680,000
Coeur D'Alene Auction

Oil On Canvas
Size: 36" x 39"

Price Range:
$5,000 to $1,700,000

Biography: Born Fresco, CA. Relocated to Utah and Arizona. Self-taught/Western.
Museums: Maynard Dixon Living History Museum, Amon Carter Museum, Museum of Art Brigham Young Univ.

GUY PENE DU BOIS

Guy pène du Bois

American (1884-1958)

Photo Copyright Artist Or Assignee.

THIRD AVENUE EL

Sold At Auction 12/2/09
$782,500
Christie's New York

Oil On Canvas
Size: 36" x 29"

Price Range:
$5,000 to $800,000

Biography: Born Brooklyn, NY. Modernist/Genre.
Museums: Metropolitan Museum, Museum of Modern Art, National Gallery of Art

MARCEL DYF

Dyf

French (1899-1985)

Photo Copyright Artist Or Assignee.

VASE DE FLEURS ET ORANGES

Sold At Auction 6/23/11
$38,340
Sotheby's Paris

Oil On Canvas
Size: 28" x 23"

Price Range:
$2,000 to $50,000

Biography: Born Paris, France. Impressionist.
Museums: Smith College Museum of Art, Musee Arlaten

Free Art Appraisals - Please Visit: www.AmericanArtAdvisor.com

GIL ELVGREN

Elvgren

American (1914-1980)

Photo Copyright Artist Or Assignee.

IT'S A SNAP

Sold At Auction 7/16/09
$215,100
Heritage Auctions

Oil On Canvas
Size: 30" x 24"

Price Range:
$2,500 to $300,000

Biography: Born St. Paul, MN. Relocated to Chicago. Illustrator (Pin-Up-Girl).
Museums: (None) Pin-Up-Girls were illustrations for Coca Cola and Covers for The Saturday Evening Post

LYONEL FEININGER

Feininger

American / German (1871-1956)

© 2012 Artists Rights Society (ARS), New York / VG Bild-Kunst, Bonn
CREDIT: Lyonel Feininger, "Angler with Blue Fish II," 1912

ANGLER WITH BLUE FISH II

Sold At Auction 6/19/06
$7,686,180
Sotheby's London

Oil On Canvas
Size: 23" x 30"

Price Range:
$15,000 to $24,000,000

Biography: Born Elizabeth, NJ. Relocated to Germany until 1936. Returned to NYC in 1937.
Museums: Metropolitan Museum, San Francisco Museum of Modern Art, Guggenheim Museum

Free Art Appraisals - Please Visit: www.AmericanArtAdvisor.com

LUCIO FONTANA

Italian (1899–1968)

CONCETTO SPAZIALE

Sold At Auction 5/10/11
$6,242,500
Sotheby's New York

Watercolor/Canvas
Size: 38" x 51"

Price Range:
$3,000 to $20,000,000

© 2012 Artists Rights Society (ARS), New York / SIAE, Rome
CREDIT: Lucio Fontana, "Concetto Spaziale"

Biography: Born Rosario Santa Fe, Argentina. Returned to Italy, 1948. Founder of Spatialism. Expressionist.
Museums: Art Institute of Chicago, Museum of Fine Arts Houston, Museum of Modern Art

E. CHARLTON FORTUNE

American (1885-1969)

Photo Copyright Artist Or Assignee.

LATE AFTERNOON, MONTEREY, 1914

Sold At Auction 12/10/07
$1,832,000
Bonhams San Francisco

Oil On Canvas
Size: 26" x 28"

Price Range:
$15,000 to $2,000,000

Biography: Born Sausalito, CA. Female California/Impressionist.
Museums: Monterey Museum of Art, Oakland Museum of Art, The Irvine Museum

Free Art Appraisals - Please Visit: www.AmericanArtAdvisor.com

SUZY FRELINGHUYSEN

S.F.

American (1911-1988)

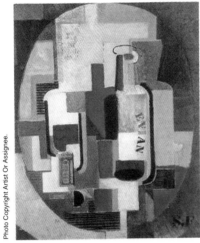

Photo Copyright Artist Or Assignee.

EVIAN

Sold At Auction 5/4/94
$92,000
Doyle New York

Mixed Media / Panel
Size: 24" x 20"

Price Range:
$3,000 to $90,000

Biography: Born Elberton, NJ. Moved to NYC around 1929. Cubist/Abstract/Modernist.
Museums: Metropolitan Museum, New Jersey State Museum, Carnegie Institute of Art

FREDERICK FRIESEKE

F.C.Frieseke

American (1874-1939)

Photo Copyright Artist Or Assignee.

IN THE GARDEN, GIVERNY

Sold At Auction 11/29/95
$1,020,000
Sotheby's New York

Oil On Canvas
Size: 32" x 32"

Price Range:
$10,000 to $2,400,000

Biography: Born Owosso, MI. Studied in New York. 1905 Moved to Paris. Impressionist.
Museums: Metropolitan Museum, National Gallery of Art, Brooklyn Museum of Art

DANIEL GARBER

Daniel Garber

American (1880–1958)

BYRAM HILLS, SPRINGTIME

Sold At Auction 12/3/03
$1,128,000
Sotheby's New York

Oil On Canvas
Size: 42" x 50"

Price Range:
$25,000 to $1,500,000

Biography: Born Manchester, IN. 1900 Located to New Hope, PA. Pennsylvania/Impressionist.
Museums: Corcoran Art Gallery, James A Michener Art Museum, Smithsonian American Art Museum

JOAQUIN TORRES-GARCIA

J.Torres.GARCIA

Latin American / Uruguay (1874–1949)

COMPOSITION

Sold At Auction: 5/30/07
$1,272,000
Sotheby's New York

Oil On Canvas
Size: 32" x 26"

Price Range:
$10,000 to $1,750,000

Biography: Born Montevideo, Uruguay. 1900's Lived in New York & Paris. Constructivist.
Museums: Barcelona Museum of Art, Museum of Fine Arts Houston, Smithsonian Hirschhorn Museum of Art

Free Art Appraisals – Please Visit: www.AmericanArtAdvisor.com

SELDEN GILE
Gile

American (1877-1947)

BELVEDERE

Sold At Auction 10/26/04
$452,000
John Moran Auctioneers

Oil On Canvas
Size: 30" x 36"

Price Range:
$5,000 to $450,000

Biography: Born Stowe, ME. 1905 moved to Oakland, CA. Self-Taught. Modernist.
Museums: Oakland Museum of CA. Monterey Museum of Art-Pacific, Utah Museum of Fine Arts

WILLIAM GLACKENS
Wl. Glackens

American (1870-1938)

TOWN PIER BLUE POINT, LONG ISLAND

Sold At Auction 11/30/95
$1,047,500
Christie's New York

Oil On Canvas
Size: 26" x 32"

Price Range:
$2,500 to $2,000,000

Biography: Born 1870 Philadelphia, PA. 1898 settled in New York. Impressionist.
Museums: Metropolitan Museum, National Gallery of Art, The White House

EMILE GRUPPE

Emile A Gruppe

American (1896–1978)

MT. MANSFIELD IN WINTER

Sold At Auction 8/1/08
$24,000
Barridoff Galleries

Oil On Canvas
Size: 25" x 30"

Price Range:
$500 to $60,000

Biography: Born Rochester, NY. 1942 Moved to Gloucester, MA. Impressionist.
Museums: Richmond Art Museum, The Washington County Museum of Fine Arts, Whistler House Museum of Art

MARSDEN HARTLEY

Marsden Hartley

American (1877–1943)

MOUNTAINS NO. 14

Sold At Auction 12/1/99
$1,542,500
Sotheby's New York

Oil On Canvas
Size: 34" x 42"

Price Range:
$7,500 to $6,500,000

Biography: Born Lewiston, ME. 1912 First Trip to Europe. Modernist.
Museums: Metropolitan Museum, Frederick R. Weisman Art Museum, Whitney Museum

Free Art Appraisals – Please Visit: www.AmericanArtAdvisor.com

CHILDE HASSAM
American (1859–1935)

Childe Hassam (signature)

Photo copyright Artist or Assignee.

DOCK SCENE, GLOUCESTER

Sold At Auction 11/29/01
$1,051,000
Christie's New York

Oil On Canvas
Size: 24" x 20"

Price Range:
$20,000 to $8,000,000

Biography: Born Dorchester, MA. 1899 Settled in New York. Impressionist.
Museums: Amon Carter Museum, Los Angeles County Museum, Metropolitan Museum

MARTIN J. HEADE
American (1819–1904)

M. J. Heade. (signature)

ORCHID AND HUMMINGBIRDS

Sold At Auction 12/3/02
$867,500
Phillips, de Pury & Co.

Oil On Panel
Size: 16" x 20"

Price Range:
$50,000 to $3,000,000

Biography: Born Lumberville, PA. Travelled throughout the U.S. (Mainly NY, CA, FL) and So America. Realist.
Museums: Brooklyn Museum of Art, Metropolitan Museum, National Gallery of Art

ROBERT HENRI

Robert Henri

American (1865-1929)

Photo copyright Artist or Assignee.

THE BLUE PLAID DRESS (ANNIE)

Sold At Auction 12/1/10
$602,500
Christie's New York

Oil On Canvas
Size: 24" x 20"

Price Range:
$2,000 to $3,600,000

Biography: Born Cincinnati, OH. Travelled to Paris and throughout the US.
Museums: Butler Institute of Art, Crocker Art Museum, Metropolitan Museum

ALBERT HERTER

ALBERT HERTER

American (1871-1950)

Photo copyright Artist or Assignee.

THE BOUVIER TWINS

Sold At Auction 11/30/99
$123,500
Christie's New York

Oil/Masonite
Size: 40" x 48"

Price Range:
$2,000 to $125,000

Biography: Born NYC. Settled in CA. Impressionist/Portraits.
Museums: High Museum of Art, Metropolitan Museum, Smithsonian American Art Museum

ALDRO HIBBARD

A.T. Hibbard

American (1886-1972)

FEBRUARY, VERMONT

Sold At Auction 9/15/06
$47,000
Skinner Inc.

Oil On Canvas
Size: 30" x 34"

Price Range:
$2,000 to $90,000

Biography: Born Falmouth, MA. 1913 Travelled to Europe. Impressionist.
Museums: Whistler House Museum of Art, Rockport Art Association, Smithsonian American Art Museum

ANTONIO HUBERTI

A. Huberti

Spanish (1907-2000)

UNTITLED

Sold At Auction 7/11/06
$2,880
Sotheby's London

Mixed Media
Size: 23" x 28"

Price Range:
$1,000 to $4,000

Biography: Lived in France. Modernist/Cubist.
Museums: (None)

OTIS KAYE

Otis Kaye

American (1885–1974)

BID AND ASK

Sold At Auction 5/24/07
$144,000
Christie's New York

Oil On Panel
Size: 12" x 15"

Price Range:
$10,000 to $450,000

Photo copyright Artist or Assignee.

Biography: Born Neemah, MI. Lived in Dresden, Germany. Then New York 1964. (Trump l'oeil/Currency.)
Museums: Sheldon Museum of Art, The Federal Reserve Board Art Collection

WALT KUHN

Walt Kuhn

American (1877–1949)

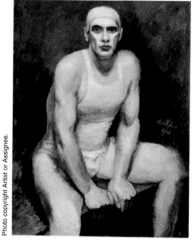

ROBERTO

Sold At Auction 5/24/01
$1,105,750
Sotheby's New York

Oil On Canvas
Size: 40" x 30"

Price Range:
$2,500 to $1,000,000

Photo copyright Artist or Assignee.

Biography: Born Brooklyn, NY. Modernist (Clowns, Portraits).
Museums: Metropolitan, National Portrait Gallery, Museum of Modern Art

WILFREDO LAM

Cuban (1902-1982)

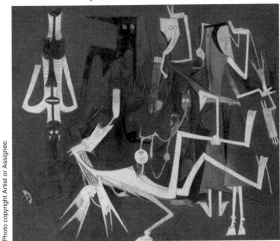

LES ABALOCHAS DANSENT POUR DHAMBALA

Sold At Auction 11/17/10
$2,154,500
Sotheby's New York

Oil On Canvas
Size: 84" x 96"

Price Range:
$5,000 to $2,200,000

Biography: Born Sagua la Grande, Cuba. Moved to Madrid. Later settled in Paris. Modernist (Spiritual Themes).
Museums: Art Institute of Chicago, Metropolitan Museum, Museum of Modern Art

JACOB LAWRENCE

American (1917-2000)

SUBWAY ACROBATS

Sold At Auction 11/30/06
$968,000
Christie's New York

Tempera/Board
Size: 20" x 24"

Price Range:
$10,000 to $2,500,000

Biography: Born Atlantic City, NJ. 1930 moved to Harlem. 1971 settled in Seattle, WA. Modernist/African American.
Museums: California African American Museum, Hirschhorn Museum & Sculpture Garden, Metropolitan Museum

HAYLEY LEVER

Hayley Lever

Australian/American (1875-1958)

MIDDAY IN THE HARBOR

Sold At Auction 9/28/10
$134,500
Christie's New York

Oil On Canvas
Size: 50" x 60"

Price Range:
$1,000 to $160,000

Biography: Born Australia. 1911 Came to America. Impressionist.
Museums: Corcoran Gallery, Metropolitan Museum, Yale Univ. Art Gallery

JOSEPH LEYENDECKER

Leyendecker

American (1874-1951)

LOVEBIRDS

Sold At Auction 5/4/11
$155,350
Heritage Auctions

Oil On Canvas
Size: 28" x 21"

Price Range:
$2,500 to $200,000

Biography: Born Germany. 1882 Moved to Chicago, then, New York. Illustrator.
Museums: Haggin Museum, National Museum of American Illustration, Metropolitan Museum

Free Art Appraisals – Please Visit: www.AmericanArtAdvisor.com

BENGT LINDSTROM

Swedish (1925-2008)

Photo copyright Artist or Assignee.

SANS TITRE

Sold At Auction 5/27/08
$53,370
Sotheby's Paris

Oil On Canvas
Size: 64" x 51"

Price Range:
$2,500 to $90,000

Biography: Born Sweden. Modernist.
Museums: Carnegie Museum, The Museé d' art Moderne, Modern Museet Stockholm

LAURENCE LOWRY

English (1887-1976)

Photo copyright Artist or Assignee.

GOOD FRIDAY, DAISY NOOK

Sold At Auction 6/8/07
$7,499,110
Christie's London

Oil On Canvas
Size: 30" x 40"

Price Range:
$6,000 to $9,000,000

Biography: Born England. Naive Genre.
Museums: Lowry Centre, Tate Gallery London, Museum of Modern Art

LUIGI LUCIONI

Luigi Lucioni

American (1900-1988)

YELLOW AND BROWN

Sold At Auction 5/19/06
$21,150
Skinner Inc. Boston

Oil On Canvas
Size: 15" x 18"

Price Range:
$2,000 to $150,000

Biography: Born Italy. 1911 came to US. Stylized Realist.
Museums: Brooklyn Museum of Art, Metropolitan Museum of Art, Whitney Museum

VICTOR MANUEL

Victor Manuel

Cuban (1897-1969)

CARNAVAL

Sold At Auction 5/26/11
$146,500
Christie's New York

Oil On Canvas
Size: 22" x 26"

Price Range:
$3,000 to $180,000

Biography: Born Cuba. Abstract/Cubist
Museums: Museo Nacional de Bellas Artes Havana

Free Art Appraisals – Please Visit: www.AmericanArtAdvisor.com

CONRAD MARCA-RELLI

American (1913-2000)

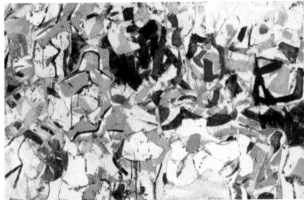

ST. CYPRIAN'S DAY

Sold At Auction 5/14/08
$1,105,000
Christie's New York

Oil On Canvas
Size: 55" x 136"

Price Range:
$2,000 to $1,000,000

Biography: Born Boston, MA. Abstract/Expressionist. (Collages).
Museums: Guggenheim Museum, Fogg Art Museum, Whitney Museum

REGINALD MARSH

American (1898-1954)

WOODEN HORSES

Sold At Auction 12/4/02
$834,500
Sotheby's New York

Tempera On Board
Size: 24" x 40"

Price Range:
$1,000 to $850,000

Biography: Born Paris, France. Settled in NJ. Urban Realist. (Genre, NYC).
Museums: Whitney Museum, Art Institute of Chicago, Metropolitan Museum

Free Art Appraisals - Please Visit: www.AmericanArtAdvisor.com

AGNES MARTIN

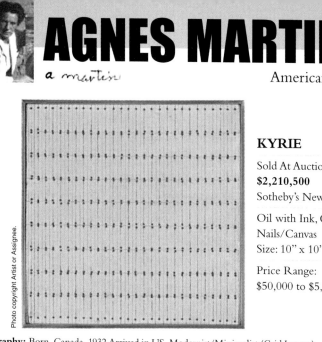

a martin

American (1912-2004)

KYRIE

Sold At Auction 5/12/10
$2,210,500
Sotheby's New York

Oil with Ink, Graphite &
Nails/Canvas
Size: 10" x 10"

Price Range:
$50,000 to $5,000,000

Photo copyright Artist or Assignee.

Biography: Born, Canada. 1932 Arrived in US. Modernist/Minimalist (Grid Images).
Museums: Whitney Museum, Metropolitan Museum, San Francisco Museum of Modern Art

LILLIAN MEESER

+ Meeser.

American (1864-1942)

Photo copyright Artist or Assignee.

STILL LIFE WITH ROSES & CHINESE PORCELAIN

Sold At Auction 12/6/07
$7,170
Heritage Auctions

Oil On Canvas
Size: 36" x 40"

Price Range:
$1,000 to $30,000

Biography: Born Ridley Park, PA. Impressionist.
Museums: Indianapolis Museum of Art, Founder, Detroit Society of Women Painters & Sculptors

BEATRIZ MILHAZES

Brazilian (1960-)

O MÁGICO

Sold At Auction 5/15/08
$1,049,000
Sotheby's New York

Oil Acrylic & Gold Leaf
on Canvas
Size: 74" x 117"

Price Range:
$25,000 to $1,000,000

Biography: Born Brazil. Modernist (Collages/Geometric Design).
Museums: Museum of Modern Art, Guggenheim Museum, Metropolitan Museum

ALICE NEEL

American (1900-1984)

JACKIE CURTIS AND RITA RED

Sold At Auction 11/11/09
$1,650,000
Sotheby's New York

Oil On Canvas
Size: 60" x 42"

Price Range:
$10,000 to $1,650,000

Biography: Born PA. 1927 Moved to NYC. Modernist (Portraits)
Museums: Metropolitan Museum, Museum of Modern Art, National Portrait Gallery

Free Art Appraisals - Please Visit: www.AmericanArtAdvisor.com

DALE NICHOLS

DALE NICHOLS

American (1904-1995)

WINTER AFTERNOON

Sold At Auction 4/8/11
$40,630
Sotheby's New York

Oil On Canvas
Size: 36" x 40"

Price Range:
$500 to $80,000

Biography: Born, Nebraska. Illustrator/Rural Regionalist.
Museums: Butler Institute of American Art, Museum of Nebraska Art, Tucson Museum of Art

KENNETH NOLAND

Kenneth Noland

American (1924-2010)

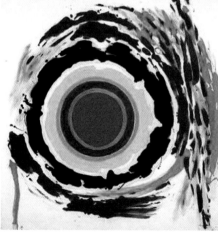

HEAT

Sold At Auction 11/14/2000
$797,750
Sotheby's New York

Acrylic On Canvas
Size: 63" x 65"

Price Range:
$5,000 to $2,000,000

Biography: Born Asheville, NC. Abstract/Expressionist.
Museums: Chrysler Museum of Art, Fogg Art Museum, Smithsonian American Art Museum

Free Art Appraisals - Please Visit: www.AmericanArtAdvisor.com

GEORGE LOFTUS NOYES

GLNoyes

American (1864-1954)

From The Authors Collection.

THE MCKINLEY HOMESTEAD

Sold At Auction 10/23/03
$19,980
Shannon's Auctioneers

Oil On Canvas
Size: 25" x 30"

Price Range:
$2,000 to $60,000

Biography: Born Ontario, Canada. Settled in Boston. Impressionist.
Museums: Addison Gallery of American Art, Museum of Fine Arts Boston, Whistler House Museum of Art

DAVID PARK

David Park

American (1911-1960)

Photo copyright Artist or Assignee.

LOUISE

Sold At Auction 5/14/08
$2,729,000
Christie's New York

Oil On Canvas
Size: 48" x 56"

Price Range:
$5,000 to $2,800,000

Biography: Born Boston, MA. Settled in CA. Modernist.
Museums: Corcoran Gallery of Art, Crocker Art Museum, San Francisco Museum of Modern Art

SAMUEL PEPLOE

Scottish (1871-1935)

Photo copyright Artist or Assignee.

TULIPS

Sold At Auction 4/22/10
$960,670
Sotheby's London

Oil On Canvas
Size: 19" x 22"

Price Range:
$7,500 to $1,500,000

Biography: Born Edinburgh, Scotland. Post-Impressionist.
Museums: Museum of Fine Arts Boston, National Galleries of Scotland, The Royal Collection, UK

ROLAND CONRAD PETERSEN

American (1926-)

Photo copyright Artist or Assignee.

APRIL PICNIC

Sold At Auction 10/11/06
$204,000
Sotheby's New York

Oil On Canvas
Size: 60" x 68"

Price Range:
$10,000 to $200,000

Biography: Born Denmark, Settled in CA. Modernist.
Museums: Hirschhorn Museum, San Francisco Museum of Modern Art, Whitney Museum

Free Art Appraisals - Please Visit: www.AmericanArtAdvisor.com

JANE PETERSON

American (1876-1965)

JANE PETERSON

GLOUCESTER HARBOR

Sold At Auction 5/18/05
$520,000
Sotheby's New York

Oil On Canvas
Size: 30" x 40"

Price Range:
$1,000 to $500,000

Biography: Born Elgin, IL. Painted in MA. Impressionist.
Museums: Brooklyn Museum, Metropolitan Museum, San Diego Museum of Art

MICHELANGELO PISTOLETTO

Italian (1933-)

UOMO CHE LEGGE

Sold At Auction 10/16/09
$550,260
Christie's London

Painted Tissue Paper on
Stainless Steel
Size: 41" x 55"

Price Range:
$5,000 to $900,000

Biography: Born Italy. Realist/Modernist.
Museums: Guggenheim, Hirschhorn Museum, Museum of Modern Art

Free Art Appraisals - Please Visit: www.AmericanArtAdvisor.com

FAIRFIELD PORTER

Fairfield Porter

American (1907-1975)

OCTOBER INTERIOR

Sold At Auction 12/1/04
$988,000
Sotheby's New York

Oil On Canvas
Size: 56" x 72"

Price Range:
$10,000 to $1,000,000

Photo copyright Artist or Assignee.

Biography: Born Winnetka, IL. Settled in Southhampton, NY. Modernized American Impressionist.
Museums: Metropolitan Museum, Smithsonian Museum of American Art, Crystal Bridges Museum

EDWARD POTTHAST

E. Potthast

American (1857-1927)

THE WATER'S FINE

Sold At Auction 5/24/07
$1,384,000
Christie's New York

Oil On Canvas
Size: 30" x 40"

Price Range:
$5,000 to $1,400,000

Biography: Born Cincinnati, OH. Located to NYC. Impressionist.
Museums: Cincinnati Art Museum, Metropolitan Museum, Museum of Fine Arts Boston

RICHARD POUSETTE-DART
American (1916-1992)

SPIRAL

Sold At Auction 11/9/11
$314,500
Christie's New York

Ink And Gouache
On Paper
Size: 23" x 29"

Price Range:
$15,000 to $700,000

Photo copyright Artist or Assignee.

Biography: Born St. Paul, MN. Located to NYC. Abstract/Expressionist.
Museums: Guggenheim Museum, Metropolitan Museum, National Gallery of Art

LEVI WELLS PRENTICE
LW Prentice
American (1851-1935)

APPLES

Sold At Auction 12/4/03
$53,780
Christie's New York

Oil On Canvas
Size: 12" x 18"

Price Range:
$2,500 to $150,000

Photo copyright Artist or Assignee.

Biography: Born Harrisburgh, NY. Realist (Still Life).
Museums: Adirondack Museum, Museum of Fine Arts Boston, Yale University Art Gallery

MAURICE PRENDERGAST

Prendergast

American (1858-1924)

COURTYARD, WEST END LIBRARY, BOSTON

Sold At Auction 5/18/04
$2,135,500
Christie's New York

Mixed Media on Paper
Size: 14" x 20"

Price Range:
$25,000 to $3,500,000

Biography: Born Newfoundland. At Ten moved to Boston. Post-Impressionist/Fauvist.
Museums: Corcoran Gallery Of Art, Metropolitan Museum, The White House.

RICHARD PRINCE

RP

American (1949-)

Photo copyright Artist or Assignee.

MAN-CRAZY NURSE #2

Sold At Auction 5/13/08
$7,433,000
Christie's New York

Acrylic & Ink-Jet Print/
Canvas
Size: 78" x 58"

Price Range:
$10,000 to $8,500,000

Biography: Born Panama Canal Zone. 1967 Moved to Los Angeles. Abstract/Expressionist.
Museums: Dallas Museum of Art, Guild Hall Museum, Ringling Museum of Art

Free Art Appraisals - Please Visit: www.AmericanArtAdvisor.com

HOVSEP PUSHMAN

Pushman

Armenian / American (1877-1966)

THE CHINESE HORSE

Sold At Auction 5/20/09
$48,800
Bonhams New York

Oil On Panel
Size: 23" x 28"

Price Range:
$15,000 to $550,000

Biography: Born Armenia. Settled in NYC. Post-Impressionist (Oriental Motif).
Museums: Metropolitan Museum, Museum of Fine Arts Boston, San Diego Museum of Art

JOSEPH RAPHAEL

JOP RAPHAEL

American (1869-1950)

FIGURES IN A GARDEN

Sold At Auction 10/29/02
$198,000
John Moran Auctioneers

Oil On Canvas
Size: 32" x 38"

Price Range:
$2,000 to $400,000

Biography: Born Jackson, CA. California Impressionist.
Museums: Oakland Museum of Art, San Diego Museum of Art, San Francisco Museum of Modern Art

Free Art Appraisals - Please Visit: www.AmericanArtAdvisor.com

NEO RAUCH

Neo Rauch

German (1960-)

STELLWERK (SIGNAL BOX)

Sold At Auction 10/16/09
$1,456,120
Christie's London

Oil On Canvas
Size: 79" x 118"

Price Range:
$10,000 to $1,500,000

Biography: Born Germany. Surrealist (Fantasy).
Museums: Los Angeles Museum of Art, Metropolitan Museum, Museum of Modern Art

---

EDWARD REDFIELD

E.W. REDFIELD

American (1869-1965)

THE OLD MILL, WASHINGTON'S CROSSING

Sold At Auction 12/7/03
$691,250
Freeman's Auctioneers

Oil On Canvas
Size: 32" x 40"

Price Range:
$15,000 to $1,000,000

Biography: Born Bridgeville, DE. 1898 Settled in PA. Bucks County Impressionist.
Museums: Carnegie Museums of Pittsburgh, Metropolitan Museum, Michener Art Museum

GRANVILLE REDMOND

Granville Redmond

American (1871-1935)

CALIFORNIA LANDSCAPE WITH OAKS, POPPIES & LUPINE

Sold At Auction 10/13/09
$517,500
John Moran Auctioneers

Oil On Canvas
Size: 30" x 40"

Price Range:
$5,000 to $550,000

Biography: Born Philadelphia, PA. 1874 Located to CA. California Impressionist.
Museums: De Young Museum, Los Angeles County Museum of Art, Irvine Museum

PERCIVAL ROSSEAU

Rosseau

American (1859-1937)

TWO SETTERS, FAYETTEVILLE, NC.

Sold At Auction 2/13/07
$210,000
William Doyle Galleries

Oil On Canvas
Size: 28" x 34"

Price Range:
$3,500 to $200,000

Biography: Born Pointe Coupee Parish, LA. Settled in NC. Realist (Dogs)
Museums: Heckscher Museum, Memorial Art Gallery, Pennsylvania Academy Of The Fine Arts

Photo copyright Artist or Assignee.

Free Art Appraisals – Please Visit: www.AmericanArtAdvisor.com

CARL SAMMONS

CARL SAMMONS

American (1883-1968)

CARMEL COAST

Sold At Auction 6/18/03
$7,170
Christie's Los Angeles

Oil On Canvas
Size: 12" x 16"

Price Range:
$500 to $12,000

Biography: Born Kearney, NE. 1913 Located to CA. California Impressionist.
Museums: De Young Museum, Santa Barbara Historical Museum, The Grace Museum

BIRGER SANDZEN

Birger Sandzen

American (1871-1954)

LATE MOON RISING

Sold At Auction 5/17/11
$262,900
Heritage Auctions

Oil On Canvas
Size: 36" x 48"

Price Range:
$2,500 to $650,000

Biography: Born in Bildsberg, sweden. Emigrated to Kansas 1894. Impressionist.
Museums: Birger Sandzen Memorial Gallery, Denver Art Museum, Museum Of Modern Art

Free Art Appraisals - Please Visit: www.AmericanArtAdvisor.com

ROLPH SCARLETT
SCARLETT.   American (1889-1984)

ABSTRACTION

Sold At Auction 9/25/08
$25,000
Christies New York

Oil On Canvas
Size: 26" x 32"

Price Range:
$1,000 to $85,000

Biography: Born in Ontario, Canada. Moved to N.Y. City in 1907. Geometric abstractionist.
Museums: Guggenheim Museum, Museum Of Modern Art, Whitney Museum

WALTER SCHOFIELD
Schofield   American (1867-1944)

RAPIDS IN WINTER

Sold At Auction 12/1/04
$456,000
Sotheby's New York

Oil On Canvas
Size: 40" x 48"

Price Range:
$4,000 to $450,000

Biography: Born Philadelphia, PA. Lived in England. New Hope Impressionist.
Museums: Art Institute of Chicago, Metropolitan Museum, Pennsylvania Academy of the Fine Arts

Free Art Appraisals - Please Visit: www.AmericanArtAdvisor.com

DONNA SCHUSTER

Donna Schuster

American (1883-1953)

THE CONCERT

Sold At Auction 4/20/10
$30,500
Bonhams & Butterfields
San Francisco

Oil On Canvas
Size: 36" x 36"

Price Range:
$2,000 to $100,000

Biography: Born Milwaukee, WI. 1913 Located to So. CA. California Impressionist.
Museums: Museum of Art at Brigham Young University, The Irvine Museum

---

KURT SCHWITTERS

Kurt Schwitters

German (1887-1948)

MZ 26,41 OKOLA

Sold at Auction 11/09/06
$576,000
Christie's New York

Collage/Board
Size: 30" x 22"

Price Range:
$10,000 to $600,000

Biography: Born Germany. Abstract (Collages).
Museums: Museum of Modern Art, Princeton University Art Museum, Sprengel Museum

---

Free Art Appraisals - Please Visit: www.AmericanArtAdvisor.com

CHARLES SCHULZ

American (1922-2000)

PEANUTS SUNDAY COMIC STRIP ORIGINAL ART 9/8/57

Sold At Auction 8/7/08
$101,580
Heritage Auctions

Mixed Media/Paper
Size: 15" x 22"

Price Range:
$500 to $125,000

Biography: Born Minneapolis, MN. Located to CA. Cartoonist.
Museums: Cartoon Art Museum. Charles M. Schulz Museum, International Museum of Cartoon Art

WILLIAM SCOTT

British (1913-1989)

BLUE STILL LIFE

Sold At Auction 11/16/07
$938,150
Christie's London

Oil On Canvas
Size: 48" x 72"

Price Range:
$6,000 to $2,000,000

Biography: Born Scotland. Located to Bath England. Abstract Expressionist.
Museums: Hirschhorn Museum, Irish Museum of Modern Art, McLean Museum of Fine Art

Free Art Appraisals - Please Visit: www.AmericanArtAdvisor.com

CHARLES GREEN SHAW

Shaw

American (1892-1974)

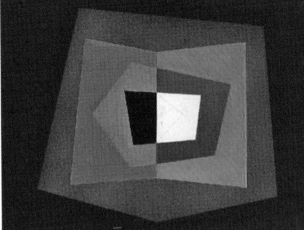

ABSTRACTION WITH BLUE, BROWN AND GREY FORMS

Sold At Auction 3/7/08
$25,000
Christie's New York

Oil On Board
Size: 16" x 20"

Price Range:
$1,000 to $60,000

Biography: Born New York City. Geometric Abstraction.
Museums: San Francisco Museum of Modern Art, Guggenheim Museum, Whitney Museum

CHARLES SHEELER

Sheeler

American (1883-1965)

STACKS IN PROCESSION

Sold At Auction 5/24/07
$1,048,000
Christie's New York

Tempera/Paper
Size: 19" x 28"

Price Range:
$10,000 to $1,000,000

Biography: Born Philadelphia, PA. Settled in Dobbs Ferry, NY. Precisionist (Structures).
Museums: Amon Carter Museum, Metropolitan Museum, National Gallery of Art

MILLARD SHEETS

Millard Sheets

American (1907–1989)

Photo copyright Artist or Assignee.

COTTON PICKERS

Sold At Auction 5/8/08
$53,780
Heritage Auctions

Oil On Canvas
Size: 36" x 40"

Price Range:
$1,500 to $55,000

Biography: Born Pomona CA. Modernist
Museums: Claremont Museum of Art, San Francisco Museum of Modern Art, Whitney Museum

WILLIAM POSEY SILVA

WILLIAM P. SILVA

American (1859–1948)

Photo Copyright Artist Or Assignee.

SPRINGTIME-CAROLINA LOW COUNTRY

Sold At Auction 6/17/03
$41,250
John Moran Auctioneers

Oil On Canvas
Size: 30" x 36"

Price Range:
$1,000 to $40,000

Biography: Born Savannah, GA. Settled in Carmel, CA. Impressionist.
Museums: Greenville City Museum of Art, Monterey Museum of Art-Pacific, Telfair Museum of Art

LEON POLK SMITH

Leon Polk Smith

American (1906-1996)

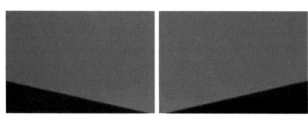

TWILIGHT

Sold At Auction 9/10/07
$85,000
Christie's New York

Acrylic/Canvas
Size: 30" x 90"

Price Range:
$4,000 to $85,000

Biography: Born Chickasha, OK. At 30 Located to NYC. Abstract.
Museums: Carnegie Museums of Pittsburgh, Guggenheim Museum, National Gallery of Art

THEODORE CLEMENT STEELE

TC Steele

American (1847-1926)

BROWN COUNTY GARDEN 1918

Sold At Auction 5/18/02
$130,000
Wickliff Auctioneers

Oil On Canvas
Size: 30" x 40"

Price Range:
$5,000 to $225,000

Biography: Born Owen County IN. Brown County IN. Impressionist.
Museums: T. C.Steele/Brown County Art Assoc., Indianapolis Museum of Art, The White House

Free Art Appraisals – Please Visit: www.AmericanArtAdvisor.com

GEORGE GARDNER SYMONS

Gardner Symons

American (1863-1930)

WINTER LANDSCAPE WITH RIVER

Sold At Auction 5/20/07
$130,000
Brunk Auctions

Oil On Canvas
Size: 45" x 60"

Price Range:
$1,500 to $130,000

Biography: Born Chicago Il. Painted in CA., NY., MA. Impressionist.
Museums: Art Institute of Chicago, Metropolitan Museum, The Irvine Museum

RUFINO TAMAYO

Mexican (1899-1991)

TROVADOR

Sold At Auction 5/29/08
$7,209,000
Christie's New York

Oil On Canvas
Size: 60" x 50"

Price Range:
$7,500 to $7,000,000

Biography: Born Mexico. Modernist
Museums: Carnegie Art Museum, Guggenheim Museum, Neuberger Museum of Art

Photo Copyright Artist Or Assignee.

ANTHONY THIEME

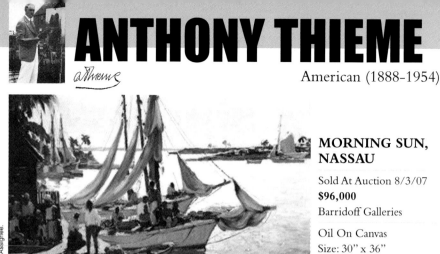

altheme

American (1888-1954)

MORNING SUN, NASSAU

Sold At Auction 8/3/07
$96,000
Barridoff Galleries

Oil On Canvas
Size: 30" x 36"

Price Range:
$2,500 to $150,000

Biography: Born Holland. 1920's Settled in U.S. (FL&MA). Impressionist.
Museums: Lightner Museum, Museum of Fine Arts Boston, Rockport Art Assoc.

WAYNE THIEBAUD

Thibaud

American (1920-)

PIES

Sold At Auction 5/9/11
$4,002,500
Sotheby's New York

Oil On Canvas
Size: 22" x 28"

Price Range:
$25,000 to $4,500,000

Biography: Born Mesa AZ. Settled in CA. Modernist.
Museums: Crocker Art Museum, Hirschhorn Museum, National Gallery of Art

---

Free Art Appraisals - Please Visit: www.AmericanArtAdvisor.com

MARION KAVANAGH WACHTEL
American (1870-1954)

Photo Copyright Artist Or Assignee.

OJAI VALLEY

Sold At Auction 12/8/04
$99,000
Bonhams & Butterfields
San Francisco

Mixed Media On Panel
Size: 20" x 32"

Price Range:
$2,500 to $100,000

Biography: Born Milwaukee WI. Settled in Pasadena,CA. California Impressionist.
Museums: Bowers Museum, Oakland Museum of California, The Irvine Museum

MARTHA WALTER
American (1875-1976)

Photo Copyright Artist Or Assignee.

LARGE YELLOW JAPANESE UMBRELLAS

Sold At Auction 5/24/06
$156,000
Sotheby's New York

Oil/Board
Size: 14" x 18"

Price Range:
$2,000 to $275,000

Biography: Born Philadelphia, PA. Studied in France. Impressionist.
Museums: National Museum of Women in the Arts, Philadelphia Museum of Art, The Terra Museum, France

FREDERICK JUDD WAUGH
American (1861-1940)

CRASHING SEAS

Sold At Auction 5/1/07
$39,000
Bonhams & Butterfields
San Francisco

Oil/Masonite
Size: 39" x 49"

Price Range:
$2,000 to $80,000

Biography: Born Bordentown, NJ. Painted in Provincetown, MA. (Seascapes). Impressionist.
Museums: Farnsworth Art Museum, Metropolitan Museum, The Newark Museum

MAX WEBER
MAX WEBER
Russian/American (1881-1961)

NEW YORK

Sold At Auction 12/3/02
$1,659,500
Phillips, de Pury & Co.

Oil On Canvas
Size: 40" x 32"

Price Range:
$2,000 to $1,650,000

Biography: Born Russia. Settled in NYC. Modernist/Cubist.
Museums: Corcoran Gallery of Art, Metropolitan Museum, Whitney Museum

WILLIAM WENDT

American (1865-1946)

DESERT GROWTH, LONE PINE

Sold At Auction 6/19/02
$185,500
Christie's Los Angeles

Oil On Canvas
Size: 25" x 30"

Price Range:
$10,000 to $550,000

Biography: Born Germany. 1906 Settled in CA. California Impressionist.
Museums: Los Angeles County Museum of Art, San Diego Museum of Art, Smithsonian American Art Museum

TOM WESSELMANN

American (1931-2004)

STILL LIFE #16

Sold At Auction 5/15/07
$3,624,000
Sotheby's New York

Mixed Media/Masonite
Size: 48" x 60"

Price Range:
$4,000 to $11,000,000

Biography: Born Cincinnati, OH. Settled in NY. Pop Artist.
Museums: Art Institute of Chicago, Dallas Museum of Art, Hirschhorn Museum

Free Art Appraisals - Please Visit: www.AmericanArtAdvisor.com

GUY CARLETON WIGGINS

Guy Wiggins NA

American (1883-1962)

THE NEW YORK STOCK EXCHANGE

Sold At Auction 12/1/05
$374,400
Christie's New York

Oil On Canvas
Size: 28" x 42"

Price Range:
$5,000 to $375,000

Biography: Born Brooklyn NY. Painted in NYC & CT. Impressionist (NYC Snow Scene).
Museums: Metropolitan Museum, National Gallery, The White House

EDWARD K WILLIAMS

Edward K Williams

American (1870-1950)

THE VALLEY OF THE WHIPPOORWILL

Sold At Auction 11/19/05
$70,000
Wickliff Auctioneers

Oil On Canvas
Size: 30" x 36"

Price Range:
$2,000 to $70,000

Biography: Born Greensburg PA. Located to Indiana. Brown County Impressionist.
Museums: The John H. Vanderpoel Art Association, Art Museum Of Lafayette, Indiana

Free Art Appraisals – Please Visit: www.AmericanArtAdvisor.com

THEODORE WORES

Theodore Wores.

American (1859-1939)

SUNSHINE AND CHERRY BLOSSOMS

Sold At Auction 4/28/04
$153,100
Christie's Los Angeles

Oil/Wood
Size: 16" x 20"

Price Range:
$2,500 to $350,000

Biography: Born San Francisco, CA. California Impressionist.
Museums: Crocker Art Museum, Los Angeles County Museum of Art, Smithsonian American Art Museum

MARGUERITE ZORACH

M.ZORACH

American (1887-1968)

THE CONNOISSEUR

Sold At Auction 5/21/03
$232,000
Sotheby's New York

Oil On Canvas
Size: 22" x 18"

Price Range:
$5,000 to $275,000

Biography: Brooklyn, NY. Modernist.
Museums: Corcoran Gallery of Art, Museum of Fine Art, Boston, Whitney Museum

Free Art Appraisals - Please Visit: www.AmericanArtAdvisor.com

CHAPTER 5

Art Styles
OF THE
Rich & Famous

Celebrity
Art
Collectors

W hat do Bill Gates, Steven Spielberg and Barack Obama have in common? Answer: They love art. You don't have to be rich to collect art, but it doesn't hurt! Billions of dollars of paintings are sold at auction every year. From 2007 to 2011, more than 20 works of art by Andy Warhol were auctioned for up to $70 million, mostly at Sotheby's and Christie's. In addition to famous art collectors, museums and corporate art collections are always seeking new acquisitions. Celebrity superstars, from Jennifer Aniston to Steve Martin, Paul McCartney, Bill Cosby, Jay-Z and Beyonce often turn to art. Whether it's a Warhol, a Van Gogh, or a Feininger, the wealthy have discovered the emotional and financial rewards of investing in prestigious paintings. Important art often appreciates in value. And it's most always saleable, privately or at auction. This makes art collecting an additional financial strategy as well as a great hobby.

David Geffen

Buying and selling valuable art is serious business. In 2006, Dreamworks co-founder David Geffen, who manages a billion dollar art collection, sold Jackson Pollock's *Number 5, 1948* and Willem DeKooning's *Woman III* for $277 million. Many experts believe Geffen's timing was perfect, and that he sold at the peak of the market. Geffen has generously pledged to donate all future revenue to

Willem DeKooning,
Woman III
© 2012 The Willem de
Kooning Foundation / Artists
Rights Society (ARS), New
York
CREDIT: Willem de
Kooning, "Woman III"

Jackson Pollock,
Number 5, 1948
© 2012 The Pollock-
Krasner Foundation /
Artists Rights Society
(ARS), New York
CREDIT: Jackson Pollock,
"Number 5, 1948"

worthy causes. After receiving a $200 million endowment, The David Geffen School Of Medicine At UCLA was re-named in his honor. Like many wealthy art collectors, David Geffen often helps people.

Microsoft Chairman Bill Gates, who has donated billions of dollars to improve education and fight world poverty, buys art to keep, although some may be donated to the Seattle Art Museum. The Gates art collection, with an estimated value of more than a billion dollars, is focused on 19th and 20th century American masterpieces like *Lost On The Grand Banks*, the last major seascape by Winslow Homer in private hands. Gates bought his Homer privately in 1998 for $36 million. In 1999, he snatched up *Polo Club* at a Sotheby's auction for a record $27.5 million. In 2001, he added the Impressionist gem *Room Of Flowers* by Childe Hassam for a neat $20 million. *Polo Club* is in the library of Gates' mansion in Medina, Washington, with *Room of Flowers* just outside in the hall. An earlier acquisition was *Distant Thunder* by Andrew Wyeth (1961), which the collector bought for $7 million in 1996. Along the way Bill Gates also added *The Nursery* by William Merritt Chase to his collection. The cost: $10 million.

Microsoft's co-founder, Paul Allen, is also an avid art collector. But while Gates, the richer of the two ($40 billion vs. $13 billion) has placed emphasis on American art, Allen has amassed a stunning group of French and European impressionists and expressionists, including Monet, Van Gogh, Signac, Renoir and Gaugin. Plus, a few American masterpieces like Roy Lichtenstein's *The Kiss* (1962). Estimated cost: *A billion or two*. In 2006, Paul Allen publicly displayed 28 paintings at

Homer: *Lost On The Grand Banks*

Bellows: *Polo Club*

Seattle's Art Experience Museum, founded by the billionaire in 2000. The exhibition included: *Rouen Cathedral: Afternoon Effect* by Claude Monet, ($13.2 million), *Concareau Morning Calm* by Paul Signac, *La Liseuse (The Reader)* by August-Pierre Renoir, *Maternite* by Paul Gaugin (sold for $39.2 million at Sotheby's), and *Four Bathers* by Pablo Picasso, a tiny but thrilling 4" x 6" Picasso, and *Orchard With Peach Trees In Blossom* by Vincent Van Gogh. Other featured artists: Jasper Johns, Edouard Manet, Paul Cezanne, Paul Seurat, Mark Rothko and Edgar Degas. Since their days at Microsoft starting in 1975, Paul Allen and Bill Gates have been collaborators and competitors. They still enjoy a healthy rivalry in art.

Hassam: *Room Of Flowers*

Signac

Gaugin

© *2012 Estate of Pablo Picasso / Artists Rights Society (ARS), New York*
CREDIT: *Pablo Picasso, "Four Bathers," 1921*

Roy Lichtenstein: *The Kiss* (exhibited at Paul Allen Museum 2006.) Photo Licensed By Corbis Images © Estate of Roy Lichtenstein

Van Gogh:
Orchard With Peach Trees

Paul Allen's museum

In 2010, a group of 57 Norman Rockwell paintings owned by Hollywood producers and longtime friends Steven Spielberg and George Lucas were exhibited at the Smithsonian American Art Museum. Spielberg (*American Graffiti, E.T.*) and Lucas (*Star Wars, Indiana Jones*)

Steven Spielberg   George Lucas

are passionate collectors of America's most famous illustrator. The value of their collections is over $100 million. When asked if he

thought the Smithsonian event might push up prices, Spielberg said he was already shocked at how high prices were. Lucas commented that he has no plans to ever sell his Rockwells so future values didn't matter to him. The auction record for a Rockwell painting is $15.4 million for *Breaking Home Ties* sold at Sotheby's in 2006. The painting was discovered behind a false wall in the Vermont home of a Rockwell friend and neighbor who bought it from the artist for $900 in 1960.

Rockwell's *Shadow Artist* (1920) *Photo licensed by ©Norman Rockwell Family Agency*

Both very private collectors, Spielberg and Lucas felt it was important to share their love of Norman Rockwell (1894-1978) with the public. From 1916 to 1963, Rockwell painted 322 covers for the Saturday Evening Post. He received $75 each for his first two paintings. During his lifetime, the artist created about 4,000 original works of art. Unfortunately, a large number were destroyed in a fire in 1943.

Rockwell: *The Flirts* (1941) Spielberg Collection. ©Norman Rockwell Family Agency

Breaking Home Ties (1954) ©Norman Rockwell Family Agency

Boy With Baby Carriage (1916) ©Norman Rockwell Family Agency

AMERICA
Loves Norman Rockwell

Life Imitates Art: Steven Spielberg mimics Norman Rockwell's *Shadow Artist* at the Smithsonian exhibition. Photo Courtesy Steven Spielberg / Marvin Levy. *(Used with Permission.)*

Norman Rockwell

President Barack Obama, Ruby Bridges, and representatives of the Norman Rockwell Museum view *The Problem We All Live With*, hanging near the Oval Office. Bridges is the girl in the painting, which appeared on the front cover of *Look Magazine* 1964. *(Official White House Photo by Pete Souza)*

Barack Obama & The White House House Art Collection

President Barack Obama has been quietly transforming the White House art collection. In June, 2009, the White House announced that the President planned to round out the permanent collection with a culturally diverse collection of African-American, Asian, Hispanic and Female artists. Prior to the Obama administration, the White House's 450-piece collection

Barack and Michelle

held predominantly 18th and 19th century works of historical significance, like Gilbert Stuart's 1797 portrait of George Washington and Thomas Moran's *Three Tetons* (1895). However, in 2007 former President George W. Bush added a cubist-inspired masterpiece titled *The Builders* (1947) by the African-American modernist Jacob Lawrence. The White House Acquisition Trust bought this painting at a Christie's auction for $2.5 million, shattering Lawrence's previous record price of under $1 million. The painting is a 20"x24" tempera on board depicting a group of hard working Americans.

The current President also decided to bring abstract and modern art into the White House, which began on his first day in office when the National Gallery loaned him Ed Ruscha's painting titled *I Think I'll* (1983) which deals with indecision. The Obamas then borrowed Richard Diebenkorn's *Berkeley No. 52* (1955), Alma Thomas's *Watusi (Hard Edge)* (1963), a tribute to Henri Matisse by the first African-American woman to have her own show at The Whitney Museum Of American Art, and Josef Albers' *Homage To The Square* (1961). *Booker T. Washington*

Jacob Lawrence: *The Builders* (1947)
© 2012 The Jacob and Gwendolyn Lawrence Foundation, Seattle / Artists Rights Society (ARS), New York
CREDIT: Jacob Lawrence, "The Builders"

President Obama straightening *Three Tetons* by Thomas Moran

President Barack Obama in Oval Office with *Avenue In The Rain* by Childe Hassam (1917)

Three Tetons by Thomas Moran
(1895)

William H. Johnson

Childe Hassam

Legend (1944-45) by
William H. Johnson
is another wonderful
African-American
painting now represented in the White House
collection.

In addition to the above paintings, the White House displays
numerous important works by American artists, such as *Avenue In
The Rain* (1917) by Childe Hassam. Behind the scenes, the collection
includes eight rarely seen Cezannes, a Monet, and a Georgia O'Keefe,
among other gems.

Steve Martin

Steve Martin is an astute and knowledgable
art collector who owns an impressive group of
paintings ranging from Picasso and Seurat to Robert
Crumb (the comic book artist), Lucien Freud, David
Hockney and Edward
Hopper. Auctioned at
Sotheby's in 1987 for $2.3
million, Hopper's *Captain
Upton's House* was
exhibited by Martin at
The Art Institute of Chicago and The
Bowdoin College Art Museum. In 1999,
Martin purchased *Hotel Window* from the
Malcolm Forbes collection for around $10
million. Forbes paid $1.3 million for it at
Sotheby's in 1987, a tidy annual return.
Hotel Window was sold by the comedian
and actor for $26.9 million in 2006, also
at Sotheby's. In 2010, Martin published a
novel titled "An Object Of Beauty", which
exposes (in a fictional format) insider
secrets of the New York art and auction
movers and shakers.

Edward Hopper: *Hotel
Window* (1956)

Edward Hopper: *Captain Upton's
House* (1927)

Paul McCartney, an artist in his own right, owns a diverse art collection including Picasso and Renoir. Paul was friends with

Paul McCartney

Vermeer

Paul McCartney and Willem DeKooning

the late Abstract Expressionist Willem DeKooning, a neighbor in the Hamptons who inspired and influenced the former Beatle's painting style. McCartney is obsessed with Jan Vermeer's 17th Century portrait of *The Guitar Player* which is in the custody of the English Heritage Foundation. He often stares at the painting at historic Kenwood House in Great Britain, and has reportedly offered $100 million to buy it!

Yellow Linda With Piano
(Photo credit Paul McCartney)

Robert Motherwell: *Throw Of Dice #17*
Art © Dedalus Foundation, Inc./Licensed by VAGA, New York, NY

Jennifer Aniston made headlines (front cover of Architectural Digest) when she purchased Robert Motherwell's *Throw Of Dice #17* (1963) for $1.2 million at Christie's in 2008. Little is known of Aniston's art collection, except that she has bought other valuable paintings from time to time.

Las Vegas and Macao casino owner Steve Wynn was bragging about his famous Picasso *La Reve* (1932) which he'd bought for around $60 million in 2001. In 2006, Wynn agreed to sell the painting to fellow billionaire collector Steven Cohen for a record

$139 million, but a not-so-minor accident happened. While swinging his arms about, Steve Wynn's poor peripheral vision caused him to shove his elbow through the canvas, piercing Marie-Therese Walter's left forearm. (Oops.) Despite a world class restoration, the

Steve Wynn

Wynn's Picasso: *La Reve*
© *2012 Estate of Pablo Picasso / Artists Rights Society (ARS), New York*
CREDIT: *Pablo Picasso, "La Reve," 1932*

"slightly imperfect" masterpiece was worth $40 million less. Cohen never completed the deal, and Mr. and Mrs. Wynn decided to hang on to the painting of Marie-Therese, Picasso's first mistress (and the mother of his daughter Maya). Steve Wynn's art collection also includes a Rembrandt bought for $33 million.

Bill Cosby

Bill Cosby And Oprah Winfrey collect African-American art, as well as other artists. A book titled "The Other Side Of Color" documents the extensive art collection of William and Camille Cosby. Artists in the Cosby collection include Joshua Johnston, Horace Pippin, Thomas Hart Benton, Reginald Marsh, Maurice Prendergast and Henry Ossawa Tanner. In 1981, the Cosbys acquired *The Thankful Poor* by Tanner for $250,000 at Sotheby's. This wonderful and moving painting was discovered in 1970 at The Pennsylvania School For The Deaf, who displayed it at the Philadelphia Museum Of Art from 1970 to 1981 before putting it up at

Oprah

auction. Henry Ossawa Tanner is America's first internationally renowned African-American artist. In 1996, Bill and Hillary Clinton purchased *Sand Dunes At Sunset, Atlantic City* by Tanner for $100,000, the first painting by an African-American artist to be included in The White House Collection. Oprah's private art collection includes works by contemporary artists Faith Ringgold and Rebecca Kinkead.

Henry Ossawa Tanner, *The Thankful Poor (1894)*

Other serious art collectors who've shelled out beaucoup bucks for major oil paintings include: Ron Lauder (Estee Lauder Cosmetics) who spent $135 million for *Portrait Of Adele Bloch-Bauer* by Gustav Klimt for his Neue Galerie museum in New York, Ted Turner, who collects Western Art and the Hudson River School (notably *Yosemite Valley* by Albert Bierstadt, sold at Sotheby's in 2003 for $7.2 million), Beyonce and Jay-Z, who are thinking of opening their own art gallery (and who own paintings by Damien Hirst and Richard Prince), Jack Nicholson, Elton John, Madonna, David Bowie, Brad Pitt, who bought a Neo Rauch for just under $1 million, and billionaire Eli Broad, who sold SunAmerica insurance company to AIG Insurance for $18 billion in 1999, and may own the best private contemporary art collection in the world.

Gustav Klimt, *Adele Bloch-Bauer* (Lauder Collection)

While the "ArtStyles Of The Rich & Famous" are exciting and newsworthy, we should point out that prohibitively expensive paintings represent only a small fraction of the vast art market. For every million-dollar painting that changes hands, thousands of modestly priced paintings find a new home. Most art collectors participate at the $5,000 to $25,000 price level. For the slightly more affluent, it's $25,000 to $250,000. Review our Artist Profile pages, refer to online auction websites, and contact the authors for free advice and appraisals. You may be pleasantly surprised at what might be hiding under that blanket, leaning against that old refrigerator or hanging on the wall of the family around the corner who inherited some old paintings from their eccentric aunt.

Ted Turner

Albert Bierstadt, *Yosemite Valley* (Ted Turner collection)

Crystal Bridges
The New American Art Museum

Asher Durand: *Kindred Spirits*

W<!---->hen Wal-Mart heiress Alice Louise Walton purchased Asher Durand's 1849 Hudson River School masterpiece *Kindred Spirits* for $35 million from the New York Public Library in 2005, the art world was stunned.

The multi-billionaire had out-bid the Metropolitan Museum of Art and the National Gallery of Art in a sealed bid auction conducted by Sotheby's, and an icon of 19th Century American art was leaving New York for, of all places, Bentonville, Arkansas. However, the painting's new home is America's freshest and most exciting art museum, Crystal Bridges, where this national treasure will still be on public display as a cornerstone of the museum's collection. Crystal Bridges promised to loan the painting to other institutions so it could be viewed across the United States. *Kindred Spirits* depicts the artist Thomas Cole and the poet William Cullen Bryant standing on a rocky ledge overlooking the Catskills. The painting is titled after a phrase in a Keats sonnet, and was commissioned by Jonathan Sturges, one of Durand's top patrons, as a gift for Bryant. It remained in the Bryant family until his daughter, Julia, donated it to the New York Public Library in 1904.

Alice Walton acquired her first piece of art when she was ten years old, a reproduction of Picasso's *Blue Nude* bought at her father's Five And Dime. She and her mother, Helen, painted watercolors on camping trips. Alice Walton serves on the board of the Amon Carter Museum in Forth Worth, Texas and is a member of the Trustees' Council of the National Gallery of Art in Washington, D.C.

There has been some criticism of Walton's enormously expensive art project. Yet the fact remains that Alice Walton has tapped into her vast $21 billion fortune to bring great American art to the attention of millions of people. Granted, Bentonville, Arkansas, headquarters to the corporate giant Wal-Mart, is not at everyone's doorstep. But the plan was to make important art accessible to people who might never visit New York City or Los Angeles, and to make Bentonville a destination. Alice Walton was born in Newport, Arkansas in 1949. Her father, Sam Walton, opened his first store (Walton's Five And Dime) in Bentonville in 1945, which is now the Wal-Mart Visitors Center. So Alice has a personal connection and fondness for the folks of Arkansas.

Alice Walton at Crystal Bridges

Opened in November, 2011, Crystal Bridges is a group of attached buildings creatively designed by the renowned architect Moshe Safdie. The museum sits on 120 acres of dogwoods, thick natural forest with three miles of walking trails, sculpture gardens

Walton's Five And Dime (Bentonville, AR)

and a series of sparkling spring-fed streams and placid ponds connected by bridges. Crystal Bridges is also a learning community for art lovers and artists. Thanks to a grant, the planned $10 admission fee has been waived. All visitors may enter the museum at no charge.

Among the 440 works of art on display at Crystal Bridges is Norman Rockwell's classic May 29, 1943 Saturday Evening Post cover *Rosie The Riveter*, sold at auction in 2002 by Sotheby's for $4.9 million to an anonymous buyer, and later sold to Walton for an undisclosed price. The 52" x 40" oil on canvas features a brawny American woman iron worker during World War II, symbolizing the feminine role in the war effort. The nationally publicized image was immediately memorable, the likeable redheaded "Rosie" depicted on her lunch break, a riveting gun in her lap as she uses a dog-eared copy of Mein Kampf as a foot stool.

Through glittering glass corridors and soaring white spaces illuminated by

Norman Rockwell: *Rosie The Riveter*
©*Norman Rockwell Family Agency*

A real life "Rosie" (1940's World War II)

natural and artificial light, masterpieces in the Crystal Bridges collection include Fairfield Porter's *Interior, October* and Arshile Gorky's *Still Life Composition*. The museum also owns works by Gilbert Stuart, Winslow Homer, Thomas Eakins, William Merritt Chase, Marsden Hartley, Georgia O'Keefe, Lyonel Feininger, Thomas Hart Benton, Stuart Davis and Charles Sheeler. Andrew Wyeth, Roy Lichtenstein and Andy Warhol help make the collection a comprehensive overview of America's first four centuries.

Alice Walton has amassed an incredible group of significant American paintings in a relatively short amount of time. "As both its supporters and detractors agree," stated the Rural Site blog, "Crystal Bridges will reshape the conversation within American museum culture and within the American arts as a whole." Carol Vogel, writing for The New York Times, commented: "The era of the world-class museum built by a single philanthropist in the tradition of Isabella Stewart Gardner, John Pierpoint Morgan Jr. and Gertrude Vanderbilt Whitney may seem to have passed, but Alice L. Walton is bringing it back." And, in the words of Abigail Esman at Forbes: "Some

Fairfield Porter: *Interior, October*

of these purchases - costing tens of millions of dollars - hang, not in private homes for the selfish enjoyment of the Walton family,

Arshile Gorky: *Still Life Composition*

but on public walls for the education and entertainment of the American people." The future success of Crystal Bridges will rise or fall on the strength of the founder's knowledge and dedication to art and its proper public exposure. In this regard, there is little doubt that the new museum is off to a good start. The authors of The Art Hunters Handbook have not yet visited Crystal Bridges, but we intend to do so soon. We can't wait to see it in person!

About The Authors
AND THE Les & Sue Fox
Art Auction Partnership

Art and numismatic experts Les and Sue Fox have written and published more than a dozen books, including *The Art Hunters Handbook* and *The U.S. Rare Coin Handbook.* Their groundbreaking *Silver Dollar Fortune Telling (1977)* advised coin collectors to invest in 19th and 20th century U.S. Silver Dollars. Working their way up from average middle class families in New York City, the Foxes managed the gold and rare coin department of an international foreign exchange bank before opening their own company in 1977. In 1988, they successfully auctioned the multi-million dollar *Amazing Gold Rarities* collection in partnership with Stack's, America's oldest rare coin dealer, in the Grand Ballroom of the Plaza Hotel.

In 2001 and 2002, two former U.S. Presidents, Gerald R. Ford and George H.W. Bush, personally provided the Foxes with thousands of autographs which were encapsulated with 1976 U.S. Bicentennial Coins, 1886 U.S. $50 Gold Eagle coins and 1992 U.S. White House Commemorative Silver Dollars. In 2001, the Foxes also reunited America's Bicentennial coin artists, Jack L. Ahr, Seth G. Huntington and Dennis R. Williams, who had not seen each other since 1976, at a special event in Palm Springs, California attended by President Gerald R. Ford.

In 1997, when their daughter Jamison (see back cover) was six years old, Les and Sue wrote *The Beanie Baby Handbook* about the hot new kids' collectible. To their pleasant surprise, the book sold 4,000,000 copies, making it a # 2 New York Times bestseller and the most successful self-published book. The Foxes' Beanie Baby collection was sold at auction for $51,000, with half of the proceeds donated to charity.

ART AUCTION PARTNERSHIP

From 2004 to 2006, while operating an art gallery which raised money for worthy causes including a kidney transplant for a young father, the Foxes created the Art Auction Partnership, a unique program for people who find or inherit valuable paintings. As explained on their website at AmericanArtAdvisor.com, the authors provide

free appraisals of original 19th and 20th century oil paintings (not prints or reproductions) which can be sold at auction. Like the artists showcased in this book, an artist's previous auction records help estimate the value of his or her work.

While auction houses do not pay the owner until after a painting is sold, the Foxes actually buy paintings as partners to sell

at auction. Offers are based on the "pre-sale auction estimate" or how much a painting is likely to bring at auction. For example, if a painting is expected to sell for $25,000, the Foxes often buy it for $15-$20,000 plus 50% of the auction profit.

Among the hundreds of artists the Foxes have recently represented in their Art Auction Program are: John Grabach, Emile Gruppe, William Trost Richards, Fern Coppedge and Hayley Lever.

Further information, please contact:
Les and Sue Fox / West Highland Art Auction Brokers
P.O. Box 36 - Midland Park, NJ 07432

Visit our websites at:
www.AmericanArtAdvisor.com or **www.EaglesOfAmerica.com**

U.S. Presidents Ford and Bush Autograph Coins For Author Les Fox

Top: President Gerald R. Ford autographs coin cards for 1976 U.S. Bicentennial Coins and 1986 U.S. $50 Gold Eagles. (2001 Photo)

Bottom: President George H.W. Bush autographs coin cards for 1992 U.S. White House Commemorative Silver Dollars. (2002 Photo)